WILLIAMS-SONOMA

# BREAKFAST

RECIPES AND TEXT
BRIGIT L. BINNS

GENERAL EDITOR
CHUCK WILLIAMS

PHOTOGRAPHS
MAREN CARUSO

SIMON & SCHUSTER • SOURCE
NEW YORK • LONDON • TORONTO • SYDNEY • SINGAPORE

# CONTENTS

## BREAKFAST SIDES

## MORNING BREADS

## WEEKEND BRUNCH

# INTRODUCTION

I cannot think of a better start to any day than a fresh, homemade breakfast. Although you may feel rushed on busy weekday mornings, it is important to take time now and then to fix yourself a warm stack of pancakes, an omelet filled with cheese and vegetables, or a wholesome bowl of oatmeal sprinkled with dried fruit and brown sugar. And there is no time like the weekend for breakfast and brunch dishes, such as fluffy waffles, savory quiches, or sticky cinnamon rolls, when leisurely mornings afford us more time to spend with family and friends.

In the pages that follow, you will find simple breakfast recipes as well as more complex brunch dishes, each accompanied by a helpful side note that explains an essential ingredient or technique. In addition, a chapter of basics in the back of the book rounds out everything you need to know to prepare a delicious breakfast. I urge you to try the recipes in this book and rediscover why a hearty, homemade breakfast is the best way to begin your day.

Chuck Williams

# THE CLASSICS

*The aroma of coffee brewing and the sound of the newspaper landing on the front steps tell you that it's time for breakfast. And whether it is a relaxed weekend or busy weekday morning, you can always rely on the classics. A cheese-filled omelet, crunchy granola that can be made in advance, and other wholesome recipes are ideal ways to greet the morning.*

# PERFECT FRIED EGGS

Place a 7- or 8-inch (18- or 20-cm) nonstick frying pan over medium heat and add the butter. When the butter has foamed and the foam begins to subside, carefully break and slip the eggs into the pan. Immediately reduce the heat to very low and cover the pan tightly. Cook slowly until the whites are firm and the yolks have begun to thicken but are not hard, about 3 minutes.

For sunny-side-up eggs, tilt the pan and spoon up the pooled butter from the edge to baste the eggs. Slide the eggs out of the pan onto warmed plates. Season to taste with salt and white pepper and serve at once.

For over-easy or over-hard eggs, use a nonstick spatula to turn the eggs over gently. For over-easy, let them cook on the second side for about 20 seconds longer before sliding them out onto warmed plates. For over-hard, let the eggs cook on the second side for 1–1½ minutes longer before sliding them out onto warmed plates. Season to taste with salt and white pepper and serve at once.

*Notes: Season the eggs only after they are cooked. Salting the eggs during the cooking process will mar the perfect yellow orb of the yolk. To double this recipe, use a large frying pan and double the number of eggs and the amount of butter or canola oil.*

MAKES 1 OR 2 SERVINGS

**2 teaspoons unsalted butter or canola oil**

**2 large eggs**

**Fine sea salt and freshly ground white pepper**

### FRIED EGG SAVVY

When preparing most egg dishes, using very fresh eggs will produce the best results. This is especially true with fried eggs. The finished fried egg will form an elongated oval, with the white closely hugging the yolk rather than spreading out around it. The advent of nonstick cooking spray and nonstick pans means that it is possible to fry an egg with virtually no fat, if desired. For a brown, lacy crust on the edges of a fried egg, do not reduce the heat to low once the egg is in the pan. Instead, keep it high and shorten the cooking time.

# CHEDDAR CHEESE AND GREEN ONION OMELET

2 green (spring) onions

4 large eggs

¼ cup (2 fl oz/60 ml) water

1 teaspoon fresh lemon juice

Fine sea salt and freshly ground pepper

1 tablespoon unsalted butter

½ cup (1 oz/30 g) shredded aged white Cheddar cheese

Thinly slice the green onions, keeping the white and tender green parts separate. Set both aside.

In a bowl, combine the eggs, water, lemon juice, ¼ teaspoon salt, and a pinch of pepper. Use a balloon whisk to beat vigorously until the color is even.

Place a 10-inch (25-cm) nonstick frying pan over medium-high heat and add the butter. When the butter has foamed and the foam begins to subside, tilt the pan to distribute the butter evenly. Pour the egg mixture through a sieve into the pan. After 30 seconds, use the edge of a nonstick spatula to push the cooked edges carefully a little toward the center, while keeping the eggs in an even layer. The uncooked eggs will flow toward the edges, and the omelet will cook more evenly. Tilt the pan and continue to move the cooked portions around the pan as necessary.

When the center of the top is thickened and there is no more standing liquid, after about 4 minutes, scatter the cheese and the white parts of the green onions evenly over the omelet. With the spatula, fold half of the omelet over to create a half circle. Let the omelet cook for about 30 seconds longer, then slip out onto a platter. Cut the omelet in half, scatter the green onion tops evenly over each portion, and serve.

*Preparation Tip: Another way to present a filled omelet is to fold it in thirds rather than in half. To do this, use the spatula to fold the top third of the omelet down over the center. Fold the bottom third up toward the center, and let cook for about 30 seconds longer before turning out onto a platter, seam side down.*

MAKES 2 SERVINGS

## OMELET VARIATIONS

Almost any cheese can be grated and used in an omelet. The key is to balance the cheese with a fresh, bracing flavor, like that of green onions or an herb such as chives, Italian (flat-leaf) parsley, or chervil. Pair cheeses with complementary flavors: chopped feta with diced avocado; soft, mild goat cheese with chervil; aged Monterey jack with cilantro. Or omit the cheese and use vegetables, such as a chopped shallot sautéed with sliced mushrooms, or diced avocado and tomatoes.

# FRENCH TOAST

**MAPLE SYRUP**
Pure maple syrup is made by boiling the clear, fresh sap of the sugar maple tree down to a rich, aromatic amber syrup. The syrup is graded according to quality and color, with the lightest syrups the most mild in flavor. A quick way to warm maple or any syrup is in the microwave. Pour the syrup into a heatproof glass or ceramic pitcher. Do not fill more than two-thirds full. Warm on 20 or 50 percent power for 1 minute. Swirl the syrup and test the temperature carefully with the tip of your finger. Warm further on low power if necessary.

In a large baking dish, place the bread slices in a single layer.

In a large glass measuring pitcher, thoroughly whisk together the milk, eggs, vanilla, Grand Marnier (if using), granulated sugar, orange zest, nutmeg, and salt. Pour evenly over the bread and let stand for 1 minute, then turn the bread over. Cover the dish with plastic wrap and let stand for at least 10 minutes or for up to 30 minutes.

In a large frying pan over medium heat, melt 1 tablespoon of the butter. When the butter has foamed and the foam begins to subside, add as many slices of bread as will fit in the pan without overlapping. When the slices are golden brown on the bottom, after about 3 minutes, carefully turn them over and cook until golden brown on the second side, about 2 minutes longer if you like custardy French toast, or about 3 minutes longer if you prefer drier French toast. Transfer the slices to a platter and keep warm in a low (200°F/95°C) oven. Melt the remaining 1 tablespoon butter and repeat with the remaining bread slices.

Transfer the French toast to individual plates, dust the tops with confectioners' sugar, and serve at once, with warm maple syrup.

MAKES 3 OR 4 SERVINGS

6 slices sturdy French or sourdough bread, about ¾ inch (2 cm) thick

1½ cups (12 fl oz/375 ml) whole milk

4 large eggs

1 tablespoon vanilla extract (essence)

1 tablespoon Grand Marnier (optional)

¼ cup (2 oz/60 g) granulated sugar

1 teaspoon grated orange zest

¼ teaspoon freshly grated nutmeg

⅛ teaspoon fine sea salt

2 tablespoons unsalted butter

Confectioners' (icing) sugar for dusting

Pure maple syrup, warmed, for serving *(far left)*

# EGGS BENEDICT

FOR THE HOLLANDAISE
SAUCE:

1 cup (8 oz/250 g) best-quality unsalted butter

2 large egg yolks

1½ tablespoons water

1 tablespoon fresh lemon juice

½ teaspoon fine sea salt

Freshly ground white pepper

4 large eggs

2 English muffins, split horizontally

Butter for spreading

4 slices Canadian bacon

2 tablespoons snipped fresh chives

To make the hollandaise sauce, in a small saucepan over medium heat, melt the butter. Set aside to cool for 5 minutes. In the top of a double boiler (page 114), combine the egg yolks, water, and lemon juice. Set the top pan over, but not touching, barely simmering water. Using a balloon whisk, begin whisking as soon as the yolks are over the heat, and whisk constantly until the mixture is light and fluffy, about 4 minutes. Remove the top pan and continue whisking away from the heat to cool slightly, about 1 minute.

Slowly drizzle the butter into the yolk mixture with one hand while continuing to whisk with the other until all the butter is absorbed, then whisk in the salt and a pinch of white pepper. Cover the pan and set aside while you poach the eggs *(right)*. The sauce can be kept warm for up to 30 minutes by placing the top pan over hot (but not simmering) water in the bottom pan of the double boiler away from the heat.

Toast the English muffins in a toaster or toaster oven. Spread the muffins with butter, then place 2 halves, cut sides up, on each plate. Keep warm in a low (200°F/95°C) oven.

In a dry, nonstick frying pan over medium-high heat, sauté the Canadian bacon just until golden and crisped to taste, 1–3 minutes on each side. Place a piece of bacon on top of each toasted muffin half. With a slotted spoon, transfer a poached egg, first resting the spoon briefly on a paper towel to blot excess water, onto each bacon-topped muffin half. Spoon a generous blanket of hollandaise sauce over each egg, sprinkle with chives, and serve.

*Note: This dish contains eggs that may be only partially cooked; for more information, see page 114.*

MAKES 2 SERVINGS

## POACHING EGGS

Use eggs that are as fresh as possible and poach only 2 or 3 eggs at a time. Bring a generous amount of water to a boil in a large sauté pan with high sides and a tight-fitting lid. Add a teaspoon of distilled white vinegar or lemon juice. Turn off the heat. Break each egg into a saucer and gently slide the egg into the water just below the surface. Alternatively, crack the eggs into an egg poacher and lower it into the water. Cover and let stand for 3 minutes for runny yolks or 5 minutes for set yolks. With a slotted spoon, transfer the eggs to a covered dish, bring the water back to a boil, and repeat.

# OATMEAL WITH DRIED FRUIT
# AND BROWN SUGAR

Warm two breakfast bowls in a low (200°F/95°C) oven.

In a small saucepan over high heat, combine the milk, rolled oats, and a pinch of salt. Using a wooden spoon, stir until the mixture begins to simmer. Reduce the heat to medium and continue stirring until the oatmeal is thickened, about 4 minutes.

Divide the oatmeal between the warmed bowls and top each serving with 1 tablespoon of the butter, if desired. Scatter each serving with half of the brown sugar and half of the diced dried fruit, and serve at once.

*Note: This recipe can easily be doubled.*

*Variation Tip: In addition to, or instead of, the diced dried fruit, add 2 bananas, peeled and diced, or ⅓ cup (2 oz/60 g) golden raisins (sultanas).*

MAKES 2 SERVINGS

**2 cups (16 fl oz/500 ml) whole or low-fat milk**

**1 cup (3 oz/90 g) old-fashioned rolled oats**

**Fine sea salt**

**2 tablespoons unsalted butter (optional)**

**1 tablespoon firmly packed light brown sugar**

**About 1 cup (6 oz/185 g) pitted dried fruit such as apricots, figs, peaches, dates, or prunes, diced**

## OATMEAL

Many oatmeal manufacturers have begun to tout the heart-healthy benefits of oats, and for good reason. A cup (8 oz/250 g) of cooked oatmeal has only 145 calories and is full of iron, magnesium, and fiber. Oats are low in saturated fat and sodium, and can help lower cholesterol levels because of their high soluble-fiber content. Several varieties of oats are available (see page 115). For the best results when making this recipe, use old-fashioned rolled oats.

# BUTTERMILK WAFFLES

2 large eggs

1¾ cups (14 fl oz/430 ml) buttermilk

¼ cup (2 fl oz/60 ml) canola oil

1 tablespoon sugar

½ teaspoon ground cinnamon

¼ teaspoon baking soda (bicarbonate of soda)

1½ cups (7½ fl oz/235 g) all-purpose (plain) flour

2 teaspoons baking powder

⅛ teaspoon fine sea salt

Butter for serving (optional)

Warmed maple syrup (page 14) for serving (optional)

2 cups (8 oz/250 g) fresh or frozen mixed berries such as blackberries, blueberries, or raspberries for serving (optional)

2 cups (16 oz/500 g) plain or vanilla yogurt for serving (optional)

Preheat a waffle iron. In a large mixing bowl, using a sturdy whisk, beat the eggs until evenly mixed. Add the buttermilk, oil, sugar, cinnamon, and baking soda. Whisk together until well combined. Add the flour, baking powder, and salt and whisk just until the large lumps disappear. The waffle batter should be a little thicker than heavy (double) cream. Transfer the batter to a large glass measuring pitcher.

When the waffle iron is hot, pour some batter evenly over the center of the grid, easing it toward, but not into, the corners and edges with a wooden spoon or heatproof spatula. Close the iron and cook according to the manufacturer's instructions until the exterior of the waffle is golden brown and almost crusty and the inside is soft, light, and springy, about 4 minutes. (The first waffle may not be perfect. Adjust the amount of batter and cooking time for the remaining waffles if necessary.) Transfer the waffle to an uncovered platter in a low (200°F/95°C) oven to keep warm while you cook the remaining waffles in the same way.

Divide the waffles among individual plates and serve at once with butter, maple syrup, berries, and/or the yogurt, if desired.

MAKES 4 OR 5 SERVINGS

BERRIES

When preparing fresh berries, pick them over, discarding any bruised or soft berries, then rinse and lay out on paper towels to dry. Berries are most flavorful and plentiful in spring and summer, but freeze well for up to 10 months. To freeze blueberries, raspberries, or blackberries, place the dried berries in a single layer on a baking sheet and freeze. When frozen, transfer the berries to freezer-proof containers. Thaw frozen berries at room temperature for about 1 hour. If necessary, transfer to a colander to drain.

# HOMEMADE GRANOLA

Preheat the broiler (grill). Place the broiler pan on the lowest rack.

In a large bowl, combine the rolled oats, wheat germ, walnuts, sesame seeds, coconut, and pumpkin seeds. Spread the mixture in an even layer on a large, rimmed baking sheet. Keeping the broiler door ajar, broil (grill), shaking the pan every 30 seconds while keeping the mixture in an even layer, until crisp and golden but not charred, 2–3 minutes. Watch the mixture carefully so it does not burn. Transfer to a large plate to cool.

In a small saucepan over low heat, combine the oil, honey, and cinnamon until warm, about 2 minutes. In a large bowl, add half of the honey mixture to the granola and toss thoroughly to combine. Add just enough of the remaining honey mixture so that the granola clumps slightly but is not soupy. Stir in the currants.

Serve the granola with milk and sliced fresh fruit, if desired.

*Note: The granola will keep in an airtight container for up to 1 week.*

MAKES 4 SERVINGS

### GRANOLA VARIATIONS

Any of the ingredients that follow may be added to the granola in balanced quantities to taste: chopped dried dates, apples, pineapples, apricots, pears, or mangoes; dark raisins or golden raisins (sultanas); dried cranberries, cherries, or blueberries; chopped almonds, hazelnuts (filberts), raw peanuts, or sunflower seeds; and/or wheat flakes or oat bran. Also try different honeys, such as lavender or orange blossom, or substitute maple syrup for the honey. When trying new additions, be sure to maintain an appealing proportion of crunchy ingredients in the final mixture.

2 cups (6 oz/185 g) old-fashioned rolled oats

½ cup (1½ oz/45 g) wheat germ

¼ cup (1 oz/30 g) coarsely chopped walnuts

¼ cup (¾ oz/20 g) white sesame seeds

¼ cup (1 oz/30 g) shredded sweetened coconut

¼ cup (1½ oz/45 g) raw hulled green pumpkin seeds

2 tablespoons canola oil

3 tablespoons honey

1 teaspoon ground cinnamon

¼ cup (1½ oz/45 g) dried currants, or to taste

Whole milk for serving

Sliced fresh fruit such as nectarines, peaches, bananas, pears, plums, mangoes, or berries for serving (optional)

# PANCAKES AND WAFFLES

*Pancakes and waffles have long been favorite staples of the breakfast table. They are a perfect match for any number of toppings: maple syrup, flavored butters, fresh berries, luscious whipped cream, or sweet preserves. Try one of the well-loved recipes in this chapter, and it will inspire you to create your own delicious combinations.*

# BELGIAN WAFFLES WITH WHIPPED CREAM AND STRAWBERRIES

**BELGIAN WAFFLES**

A Belgian waffle and a standard American waffle are substantially different. An American waffle gains its rising power solely from baking powder. A Belgian waffle is raised with yeast, which adds a tangy flavor, and beaten egg whites, which lend a light texture.

Belgian waffles are also much thicker than American waffles, which is why they must be made in a Belgian waffle iron. The resulting deeper holes accommodate luscious toppings such as berries and whipped cream.

The night before you plan to serve the waffles, in a large bowl, whisk together the flour, granulated sugar, salt, and yeast. In a small saucepan over medium-high heat, combine the whole milk and sparkling mineral water and heat to lukewarm (105°F/40°C). Whisk in the melted butter and vanilla. Pour into the dry ingredients and whisk until smooth. Cover tightly and let stand overnight at cool room temperature.

The next morning, preheat a Belgian waffle iron. Whisk the egg yolk into the batter. In a large, clean bowl, using an electric mixer on high speed, beat the egg whites and the cream of tartar until soft peaks form. Thoroughly stir about one-third of the beaten whites into the batter, then fold in the remaining whites, without overmixing. Transfer to a large glass measuring pitcher.

When the waffle iron is hot, pour ¾–1 cup (6–8 fl oz / 180–250 ml) of the batter into each waffle section and spread with a wooden spoon so the grids are evenly covered. Close the iron and cook according to the manufacturer's instructions until the waffle exterior is golden brown and the inside is light and springy, 4–5 minutes. (The first waffle may not be perfect. Adjust the amount of batter and cooking time if necessary.)

Meanwhile, in a chilled bowl, combine the cream and superfine sugar. Using the mixer on medium-high speed, beat until soft peaks form, about 2 minutes. Cover the bowl and refrigerate.

As soon as the waffle is ready, remove it from the iron, divide, and transfer to a warmed individual plate. Dust with confectioners' sugar, if using, smother each portion with some of the strawberries, and top with a dollop of the whipped cream. Cook the remaining waffles as guests sit down to the first batch.

MAKES 4 OR 5 SERVINGS

1 cup (5 oz / 155 g) all-purpose (plain) flour, sifted

1 tablespoon granulated sugar

¼ teaspoon fine sea salt

½ teaspoon active dry yeast

½ cup (4 fl oz / 125 ml) whole milk

½ cup (4 fl oz / 125 ml) sparkling mineral water

¼ cup (2 oz / 60 g) unsalted butter, melted and still warm

½ teaspoon vanilla extract (essence)

1 large egg yolk

2 large egg whites

Pinch of cream of tartar

½ cup (4 fl oz / 125 ml) heavy (double) cream

1 tablespoon superfine (caster) sugar

Confectioners' (icing) sugar for dusting (optional)

1½ cups (6 oz / 185 g) sliced strawberries for serving

# PUMPKIN-PECAN WAFFLES
# WITH MAPLE-CRANBERRY BUTTER

FOR THE MAPLE-CRANBERRY
BUTTER:

½ cup (2 oz/60 g) fresh or
thawed frozen cranberries

¼ cup (2¾ oz/80 g) pure
maple syrup

1 cup (8 oz/250 g)
unsalted butter, at room
temperature

1 cup (5 oz/155 g)
all-purpose (plain) flour,
sifted

1 tablespoon firmly packed
dark brown sugar, sifted

1 teaspoon baking powder

¼ teaspoon fine sea salt

1¼ cups (10 fl oz/310 ml)
whole milk

1 large egg, lightly beaten

1½ tablespoons unsalted
butter, melted

⅔ cup (5½ oz/170 g)
pumpkin purée *(far right)*

⅓ cup (1½ oz/45 g)
coarsely chopped pecans

Warmed maple syrup
(page 14) for serving
(optional)

To make the maple-cranberry butter, in a small saucepan over low heat, combine the cranberries and maple syrup and cook, stirring frequently, until the cranberries have softened and popped, about 5 minutes. Let cool, then place in a large bowl and add the butter. Beat with a wooden spoon until just combined. Cover the maple-cranberry butter and refrigerate until ready to serve.

Preheat a waffle iron. In a large bowl, whisk together the flour, brown sugar, baking powder, and salt until well mixed. In a large glass measuring pitcher, whisk together the milk, egg, and butter. Stir the milk mixture and the pumpkin purée into the dry ingredients until just blended. The batter may be slightly lumpy; do not overmix. Stir in the pecans and transfer the batter back to the pitcher.

When the waffle iron is hot, pour some batter evenly over the center of the grid, easing it toward, but not into, the corners and edges with a wooden spoon or heatproof spatula. Close the iron and cook according to the manufacturer's instructions until the exterior of the waffle is golden brown and almost crusty and the inside is soft, light, and springy, about 4 minutes. (The first waffle may not be perfect. Adjust the amount of batter and cooking time for the remaining waffles if necessary.) Transfer each waffle to an uncovered platter in a low (200°F/95°C) oven to keep warm while you cook the remaining waffles in the same way.

Divide the waffles among warmed individual plates. Using a small ice-cream scoop, place a ball of cranberry butter on top of each waffle and serve at once with warm maple syrup, if desired.

MAKES 3 OR 4 SERVINGS

### PUMPKIN PURÉE
To make your own purée, use 1 large or 2 medium Sugar Pie or other eating pumpkins. Cut out the stem, quarter the pumpkin lengthwise, and scoop out the seeds. In a preheated 400°F (200°C) oven, bake the quarters, cut sides down, in a shallow roasting pan, with a little water in the bottom, until tender, about 1 hour. Let cool, scrape the flesh from the peels, and force through a medium-mesh sieve or the medium disk of a food mill. Freeze any leftover purée for up to 2 months.

# BLUEBERRY PANCAKES

In a large bowl, sift together the flour, sugar, baking powder, baking soda, and salt. Stir until well mixed and make a well in the center. Pour the eggs, the milk, and the 2 tablespoons melted butter into the well, then gradually whisk from the center outward, until the ingredients are well combined but still a little lumpy; do not overmix the batter, or the pancakes will be heavy. Very gently stir in the blueberries. The batter will be quite thick.

Preheat a nonstick or cast-iron griddle over medium-high heat until a drop of water flicked onto the surface dances and evaporates instantly. Brush the griddle with a little of the ¼ cup melted butter. Slowly ladle a scant ¼ cup (2 fl oz/60 ml) of the batter onto the griddle, centering the ladle over the batter so it spreads out into a circle on its own. If necessary, use the bottom of the ladle to nudge the batter into a perfect circle. Continue ladling out the batter to make as many pancakes as you can without letting them touch. If they do touch, separate with the edge of a spatula.

When the pancakes have begun to bubble in the center and a few of the bubbles have popped and the undersides are golden, after about 2 minutes, use the spatula to flip them. Cook until the second side is golden, about 1 minute longer, then transfer to a platter in a low (200°F/95°C) oven to keep warm. Cook the remaining pancakes in the same way, adding butter to the griddle as needed.

Transfer the pancakes to warmed individual plates and serve at once, topped with whipped butter, if desired, and warm syrup.

MAKES 3 OR 4 SERVINGS

## BLUEBERRIES
The color blue is rare in food, but blueberries are a delicious exception. Take care when using blueberries since the intense color can bleed into your pancake batter and turn it blue-gray. One solution is not to let frozen blueberries thaw before you stir them into the batter. Fresh blueberries bleed less than frozen. A large percentage of the blueberries in the United States come from Maine, where they are the state berry.

2 cups (10 oz/315 g) all-purpose (plain) flour

2 tablespoons sugar

2 teaspoons baking powder

1½ teaspoons baking soda (bicarbonate of soda)

½ teaspoon fine sea salt

2 large eggs, lightly beaten

1¾ cups (14 fl oz/430 ml) whole milk

2 tablespoons unsalted butter, melted and cooled, plus ¼ cup (2 fl oz/60 ml) melted for frying

1½ cups (6 oz/185 g) fresh or frozen blueberries *(far left)*

Whipped butter for serving (optional)

Warmed maple syrup (page 14) or boysenberry syrup for serving

# GERMAN APPLE PANCAKE

5 large eggs

2 teaspoons vanilla extract (essence)

½ cup (4 oz/125 g) plus 1 tablespoon granulated sugar

⅓ cup (2 oz/60 g) all-purpose (plain) flour

1 teaspoon baking powder

⅛ teaspoon fine sea salt

1½ tablespoons unsalted butter

2 large, tart apples, peeled, cored, and cut into wedges ½ inch (12 mm) thick

1 teaspoon ground cinnamon

1 tablespoon confectioners' (icing) sugar (optional)

¾ cup (3 oz/90 g) fresh raspberries (optional)

¼ cup (2 oz/60 g) crème fraîche (page 99)

In a blender, combine the eggs, the vanilla, and the ½ cup granulated sugar and blend until combined, about 5 seconds. Add the flour, baking powder, and salt and mix until smooth, about 10 seconds more.

Preheat the oven to 375°F (190°C). Place a 10-inch (25-cm) ovenproof, nonstick frying pan over medium heat and add the butter. When the butter has foamed and the foam has subsided, add the apples and sauté, stirring occasionally, until softened, 4–5 minutes. Sprinkle the apples with the cinnamon and the remaining 1 tablespoon granulated sugar. Stir together and sauté until the apples are glazed and the edges are slightly translucent, about 2 minutes longer.

Spread the apples evenly in the frying pan and pour the batter slowly over the top, so the apples stay in place. Reduce the heat to medium-low and cook until the bottom is firm, about 8 minutes. Transfer the pan to the oven and cook until the top of the pancake is firm, about 10 minutes longer.

Remove from the oven, invert a flat serving plate over the frying pan, and then, holding the pan and plate together, invert them together and lift off the pan. Cut the pancake into 3 or 4 wedges and transfer to individual plates. If desired, sprinkle each portion with confectioners' sugar and scatter with a few raspberries. Place a dollop of crème fraîche on top and serve at once.

MAKES 3 OR 4 SERVINGS

GERMAN APPLE PANCAKES

The traditional way to make this beloved German dish, known as *Apfelpfannkuchen,* is to flip the pancake in the pan while it is on the stove top to cook the second side. This can be a tricky maneuver since you don't want to displace the apples. Here, the pancake is finished in the oven, which is an easier option. Most other European pancakes are also cooked at least partially in the oven (see Swedish Pancake, page 34). European pancakes often contain pieces of fruit or meat, such as the apples used here or the ham called for in Swedish pancakes.

# SWEDISH PANCAKE

In a large bowl, beat together the flour, milk, eggs, butter, sugar, nutmeg, and salt. Cover the bowl and let the batter stand for at least 1 hour to allow the flour to expand. (The batter can be refrigerated for up to 12 hours before cooking, if desired.)

Preheat the oven to 425°F (220°C). Place a 9- or 10-inch (23- or 25-cm) cast-iron frying pan over medium-high heat and add the oil. Swirl around or brush to coat about halfway up the sides of the pan. When the oil is hot, add the ham and stir until crisp and golden, about 4 minutes. Spread the ham evenly in the frying pan, leaving a 1-inch (2.5-cm) border around the edges. Pour the batter slowly over the top, so the ham stays in place. Transfer the pan to the oven and bake until the pancake is deep, golden brown and very puffy around the edges, 10–15 minutes.

Cut the pancake into 3 or 4 wedges and serve at once, topped with a spoonful of lingonberry preserves or a dollop of mustard.

MAKES 3 OR 4 SERVINGS

¾ cup (4 oz/125 g) all-purpose (plain) flour

¾ cup (6 fl oz/180 ml) whole milk

3 large eggs

1½ tablespoons unsalted butter, melted

1 teaspoon sugar

⅛ teaspoon freshly grated nutmeg

Pinch of fine sea salt

2 teaspoons canola oil

¼ lb (125 g) flavorful cooked ham such as country ham or Black Forest ham, diced

Lingonberry preserves or Dijon mustard for serving

LINGONBERRIES

These small, red fruits, grown on bushes that are less than a foot tall, are made into jams, jellies, and preserves, and are popular in Scandinavian cooking, often to accompany game. Lingonberries are also delicious as a filling for crepes and a garnish for waffles, pancakes, and other sweet breads and cakes. A relative of the cranberry, the tart berry is also known as cow berry, partridge berry, dry-ground cranberry, and fox berry. The name *lingonberry* originated in Sweden, but the Pacific Northwest now grows more lingonberries than any other region in the world.

# GINGER-PEAR PANCAKES

1¼ cups (6½ oz/200 g) all-purpose (plain) flour

1 teaspoon baking powder

½ teaspoon baking soda (bicarbonate of soda)

¼ teaspoon fine sea salt

2 tablespoons raw or turbinado sugar

1 large egg, lightly beaten

1¼ cups (10 fl oz/310 ml) whole milk

1 teaspoon firmly packed, grated fresh ginger with juice

2 tablespoons unsalted butter, melted, plus ¼ cup (2 fl oz/60 ml) melted for frying

1 ripe Anjou or other sweet pear, peeled, cored, and cut into ⅜-inch (1-cm) dice

½ cup (5 oz/155 g) ginger preserves or marmalade, warmed

In a bowl, sift together the flour, baking powder, baking soda, and salt. Whisk in the sugar, then make a well in the center. Pour the egg, milk, grated ginger with juice, and 2 tablespoons melted butter into the well, then gradually whisk from the center outward until the ingredients are well combined but still a little lumpy; do not overmix, or the pancakes will be heavy. Gently stir in the pear. The batter will be fairly thin.

Preheat a nonstick or cast-iron griddle over medium-high heat until a drop of water flicked onto the surface dances and evaporates instantly. Brush the griddle with a little of the ¼ cup melted butter. Slowly ladle a scant ¼ cup (2 fl oz/60 ml) of the batter onto the griddle, centering the ladle over the batter so it spreads out into a circle on its own. Continue ladling out the batter to make as many pancakes as you can without letting them touch. If they do touch, separate with the edge of a spatula.

When the pancakes have begun to bubble in the center and a few of the bubbles have popped and the undersides are golden, after about 2 minutes, use the spatula to flip them. Cook until the second side is golden, about 1 minute longer, then transfer to a platter in a low (200°F/95°C) oven to keep warm. Cook the remaining pancakes in the same way, adding butter to the griddle as needed.

Transfer the pancakes to warmed individual plates and serve at once, topped with a dollop of warmed ginger preserves or ginger marmalade.

MAKES 3 OR 4 SERVINGS

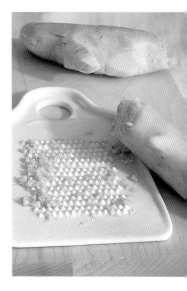

GINGER
Fresh ginger brings a lively, warm, spicy flavor to these pancakes. In the market, look for ginger that is hard and heavy, with an unbroken peel that is thin, pale, and smooth. To prepare fresh ginger, peel it with a vegetable peeler or paring knife. Once peeled, it is often grated to capture its flavor without its fibrous texture. Porcelain ginger graters, specially designed to let you use the aromatic juice and flesh without the tough fibers, are sold in Asian markets and specialty cookware stores. You can also use the smallest rasps on a metal grater.

# EGGS

*An egg is one of nature's perfect designs: protein, vitamins, minerals, and flavor, all in one simple package. Nowhere is the egg more appreciated than at the breakfast table. Make omelets with fresh herbs or asparagus for elegant presentations. Try huevos rancheros or a frittata for heartier fare. Scrambled, soft-boiled, or coddled, eggs also make ideal morning comfort food.*

# SOUFFLÉED OMELET WITH FINES HERBES

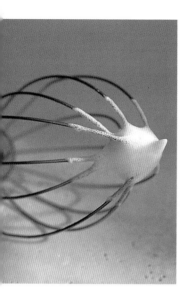

**SOUFFLÉED OMELETS**

The souffléed omelet, or fluffy omelet, is a hybrid of two popular egg preparations, the omelet and the soufflé. It takes advantage of the extra loft achieved when egg whites are whipped separately, then gently folded into the yolks. To check the consistency of beaten egg whites, remove the whisk from the bowl and turn it upright. Soft peaks on the beaters' tips will fall gently to one side, while stiff peaks will hold their shape. Stiff egg whites should not be dry or grainy and should not slip when the bowl is tilted, a sign that they have been overbeaten.

Preheat the oven to 350°F (180°C). In a large, spotlessly clean bowl, combine the egg whites, water, and cream of tartar. Using an electric mixer on high speed, beat until stiff peaks form when the beaters are lifted *(left)*. Set aside.

In a small bowl, beat the egg yolks, ¼ teaspoon salt, and a pinch of pepper until pale and thickened, about 1 minute. Stir the Parmesan, chervil, chives, parsley, and tarragon into the yolks until well blended.

Place a 10-inch (25-cm) ovenproof, nonstick frying pan over medium-high heat and add the butter. While it is melting, working quickly and using a large rubber spatula, gently fold the yolk mixture into the egg whites, taking care not to crush too much air out of the egg whites.

When the butter has foamed and the foam begins to subside, tilt the pan to distribute the butter evenly. Scoop the egg mixture into the pan and smooth the surface gently with a nonstick spatula. Reduce the heat to medium and cook until the omelet is puffed and the bottom is golden, about 5 minutes. Transfer the pan to the oven and bake until the omelet is firm in the center, about 7 minutes longer.

Remove from the oven and, using the spatula, loosen the edges of the omelet, then slide it onto a platter. Cut the omelet in half or into 3 wedges and serve at once.

*Note: A classic French blend of herbs, fines herbes consists of chervil, chives, parsley, and tarragon.*

MAKES 2 OR 3 SERVINGS

**4 large eggs, separated (page 96)**

**¼ cup (2 fl oz/60 ml) water**

**½ teaspoon cream of tartar**

**Fine sea salt and freshly ground pepper**

**2 tablespoons grated Parmesan cheese**

**1 tablespoon minced fresh chervil**

**1 tablespoon finely snipped fresh chives**

**1 tablespoon minced fresh flat-leaf (Italian) parsley, plus sprigs for garnish**

**1 tablespoon minced fresh tarragon**

**2 teaspoons unsalted butter**

# ASPARAGUS AND GRUYÈRE OMELET

5 large eggs

¼ cup (2 fl oz/60 ml) water

1 teaspoon fresh lemon juice

Fine sea salt and freshly ground pepper

1 tablespoon unsalted butter

1 teaspoon finely snipped fresh chives (optional)

3 tablespoons finely shredded Gruyère cheese

12 medium asparagus tips, about 2 inches (5 cm) long, parboiled *(far right)*

In a small bowl, whisk together the eggs, water, lemon juice, ¼ teaspoon salt, and a pinch of pepper until the color is even.

Place a 10-inch (25-cm) nonstick frying pan over medium-high heat and add the butter. When the butter has foamed and the foam begins to subside, tilt the pan to distribute the butter evenly. Pour the egg mixture through a sieve into the pan. Scatter the surface evenly with the chives, if using. After 30 seconds, use the edge of a nonstick spatula to push the cooked edges carefully a little toward the center, while keeping the eggs in an even layer. The uncooked eggs will flow gently toward the edges, and the omelet will cook more evenly. Continue to tilt the pan and move the cooked portions around the pan as necessary.

When the center of the top is thickened and there is no more standing liquid, after about 4 minutes, scatter the cheese evenly over the omelet and distribute the asparagus tips on one half of the omelet. With the spatula, lift up the half without the asparagus and fold it over to create a half circle. Let the omelet cook for about 30 seconds longer, then slip out onto a platter.

Cut the omelet in half or into 3 wedges. Serve at once.

*Note: To use the remaining asparagus after the tips have been removed, snap off the woody ends from the stalks. Parboil (right) the trimmed stalks until tender, 5–7 minutes. Coarsely chop and add to a frittata (page 51), scrambled eggs, or soup.*

MAKES 2 OR 3 SERVINGS

PARBOILING

This method of partially cooking food in boiling water is often a preparatory step before finishing with another cooking method. The asparagus tips in this recipe must be parboiled because their stay in the pan with the eggs is too brief to cook them completely. To parboil the asparagus, bring a small saucepan three-fourths full of salted water to a boil. Add the asparagus tips and parboil until tender, about 3 minutes. Drain and rinse under cold running water until thoroughly cooled. Transfer to a paper towel–lined plate to drain and set aside.

# SCRAMBLED EGGS WITH
# SMOKED SALMON AND AVOCADO

**HOT-PEPPER SAUCE**

Sriracha sauce is a hot-pepper sauce from Thailand that is now widely available. Sun-ripened serrano chiles and plenty of garlic are ground to a smooth paste, lending the sauce a mellow, yet unabashedly spicy flavor. Keep in mind that a little of this sauce goes a long way as a condiment in soups, on eggs, pasta, and pizza—and even on hamburgers and hot dogs. Sriracha is sold in a squeeze bottle, which should be shaken well before the sauce is used. A Latin American chile sauce may be substituted.

In a bowl, whisk together the eggs, cream, and ½ teaspoon salt until very smooth.

Place a large, nonstick frying pan over high heat. Add the butter. When the butter has foamed and the foam begins to subside, tilt the pan to distribute the butter evenly. Pour all of the egg mixture into the pan and let the eggs cook undisturbed for 30 seconds. Stir gently with a wooden spoon, bringing the partially cooked edges in toward the center. Let cook undisturbed for 30 seconds longer, then stir again. Remove the pan from the heat and let stand for 1 minute longer, then stir again gently.

Divide the smoked salmon evenly between 2 individual plates, arranging it in an even layer. Spoon half of the scrambled eggs onto the center of each plate, and arrange the avocado slices alongside the eggs. Sprinkle the eggs with a few drops of hot sauce and serve at once.

*Note: Before cooking the eggs, be sure to beat them vigorously to incorporate lots of air. This is a key to achieving super-lofty, creamy, and soft scrambled eggs.*

MAKES 2 SERVINGS

5 large eggs

1 cup (8 fl oz/250 ml) heavy (double) cream or half-and-half (half-cream)

Fine sea salt

1 tablespoon unsalted butter

2 oz (60 g) thinly sliced smoked salmon

½ ripe avocado, sliced

Thai Sriracha or other hot-pepper sauce

# CODDLED EGGS WITH CHIVES AND CREAM

2 tablespoons heavy
(double) cream

1 teaspoon minced cooked
ham (optional)

1½ tablespoons minced
fresh spinach leaves

Fine sea salt and freshly
ground pepper

2 large eggs

1 teaspoon finely snipped
fresh chives

2 slices bread, toasted
and buttered (page 48),
for serving

Pour water to a depth of 1½ inches (4 cm) into a wide, deep saucepan and bring to a boil over high heat.

Meanwhile, place 1 tablespoon of cream in the base of each of 2 covered egg coddlers or standard 4– to 5–fl oz (125- to 160-ml) ramekins (see Notes) and swirl the cream to coat about halfway up the inside walls. Add half each of the ham, if using, and the spinach to each coddler. Sprinkle a tiny pinch of salt and pepper into each one. Carefully break an egg into each coddler, being careful not to break the yolk. Cover the coddlers with their tops (or with small squares of heavy-duty aluminum foil if using ramekins).

Carefully place the coddlers in the saucepan of boiling water. Reduce the heat so that the water simmers briskly and cover the saucepan. Simmer for 6 minutes, then use an oven mitt to transfer the coddlers to individual plates.

Remove the lids from the coddlers, season with additional salt and pepper to taste, and sprinkle with the chives. Serve at once with warm, buttered toast.

*Notes: If using standard ramekins to coddle eggs, make sure the white is set and the yolk still jiggles before serving. Coddled eggs may be only partially cooked; for more information, see page 114.*

*Serving Tip: To turn the egg out onto the toast, omit the cream and spray the coddler or ramekin with nonstick cooking spray.*

MAKES 2 SERVINGS

### CODDLING

Coddling is a very gentle cooking method that uses simmering water to insulate food from the direct heat of the stove. This method allows you to cook food, especially eggs, slowly and evenly, yielding eggs that have been cooked just enough so they are no longer raw but still extremely soft. Egg coddlers, a type of lidded glass or porcelain dish, are made especially for this technique. You can also coddle the eggs in standard ramekins.

# SOFT-BOILED EGGS WITH TOAST STRIPS

## TOAST

When it comes to making toast, there is an abundance of choices. For a savory bite, choose sourdough or rye bread; for a rustic and wholesome option, try pumpernickel or multigrain bread. For pure comfort, choose an egg bread such as challah or Brioche (page 86). To avoid tearing the crusty slices as you spread them with butter, soften the butter for 30 to 40 minutes before serving time. Toast can be made in a toaster, but it is sometimes easier to use a broiler (be sure to set a timer and check every 1 or 2 minutes).

Have ready 2 egg cups placed on 2 small plates, as well as 2 teaspoons for serving (the bowls of the spoons must be small enough to fit inside the tops of the egg shells).

Toast the bread slices until golden *(left)*, then spread evenly with the butter, and cut lengthwise into strips about ¾ inch (2 cm) wide. Keep the toast strips warm in a low (200°F / 95°C) oven while you cook the eggs.

Bring a saucepan three-fourths full of water to a boil over high heat. One at a time, place the unbroken eggs on a large, slotted spoon, then gently lower to the bottom of the pan, and ease the spoon away (be careful at this point not to crack the eggs). Reduce the heat so the water barely simmers and cook for 3 minutes. Remove the eggs with the spoon and place under cold running water for 1 minute.

Place each egg, pointed end down, into an egg cup. To eat, use a knife to crack and remove the top part of the egg. Lift off the top and sprinkle a few grains of salt inside each egg. Eat at once, dipping the toast strips into the runny egg yolk inside. Use the teaspoons to scoop out the egg whites.

*Note: This dish contains eggs that may be only partially cooked; for more information, see page 114.*

MAKES 2 SERVINGS

4 slices white or whole-wheat (wholemeal) bread, crusts removed

2 tablespoons butter, softened

2 extra-large or jumbo eggs

Fine sea salt

# CHICKEN SAUSAGE, SUN-DRIED TOMATO, AND ZUCCHINI FRITTATA

1 lb (500 g) fresh chicken sausage, casings removed

¼ cup (1 oz/30 g) fine dried bread crumbs (page 114)

¾ lb (375 g) small, firm zucchini

2 large cloves garlic

1 tablespoon olive oil

2 tablespoons dry white wine (optional)

2 tablespoons finely shredded fresh basil leaves

½ cup (3 oz/90 g) cooked macaroni, tossed with 1½ teaspoons olive oil

6 dry-packed, sun-dried tomato halves, soaked in very hot water for 20 minutes, squeezed dry, and finely chopped

¾ cup (3 oz/90 g) coarsely grated Parmesan cheese

Fine sea salt and freshly ground pepper

9 large eggs

1 cup (8 fl oz/250 ml) whole milk

2 teaspoons Dijon mustard

In a nonstick or cast-iron frying pan over medium-low heat, cook the sausage, breaking up the meat, until no trace of pink remains, about 6 minutes. (Do not overcook, or the sausage will be dry.) Using a slotted spoon, transfer to a paper towel–lined plate to drain. Discard any fat from the pan.

Preheat the oven to 350°F (180°C). Grease a 9-inch (23-cm), nonstick springform pan with butter and coat it with the bread crumbs, shaking out the excess.

Trim and coarsely grate the zucchini. Mince the garlic. Return the frying pan to medium heat and add the olive oil. Add the zucchini and sauté until bright green, about 2 minutes. Add the garlic and cook for about 1 minute. Add the white wine, if using, and cook for a few minutes more until evaporated. Remove from the heat and stir in the basil.

In a bowl, combine the macaroni, tomatoes, cheese, ¾ teaspoon salt, and ½ teaspoon pepper. Toss to mix. Spoon the sausage into the springform pan in an even layer. Spoon the zucchini mixture over the sausage and top with the pasta mixture. In a bowl, whisk together the eggs, milk, and mustard until well blended. Pour the egg mixture evenly over the ingredients. Cover the pan with aluminum foil and bake until the outer 2 inches (5 cm) are firm, about 30 minutes. Remove the foil and cook until golden brown, about 40 minutes longer.

Let cool on a rack for 20 minutes, then loosen the sides with a small knife. Remove the sides, place a platter upside down on top of the frittata, and invert. Cut the frittata into wedges and serve.

MAKES 6 SERVINGS

## FRITTATA VARIATIONS

An extremely versatile Italian egg dish, a frittata can contain many savory ingredients, as long as they require little or no cooking or have been precooked. A frittata is the perfect place for leftovers to make a repeat appearance in the next day's breakfast or lunch. Try it with about ½ cup (3 oz/90 g) leftover cooked pasta and 2–3 cups (12–18 oz/ 375–560 g) cooked diced vegetables such as ripe tomatoes, roasted red bell peppers (capsicums), onions, potatoes, and mushrooms.

# HUEVOS RANCHEROS

If the tortillas are still fresh, spread them in a single layer on a work surface and let them dry out for 5 minutes. Meanwhile, in a wide, shallow saucepan, warm the sauce.

In a large cast-iron or nonstick frying pan over medium-high heat, warm the ¼ cup (2 fl oz/60 ml) oil. One at a time, fry the tortillas, turning over, to soften, about 5 seconds on each side. Using tongs, transfer to paper towels to drain and keep warm in a low (200°F/95°) oven.

Reduce the heat to medium-low and wait a couple of minutes for the frying pan to cool down. Break 4 of the eggs into the pan and fry them slowly until the whites are set and the yolks have begun to thicken but are not hard (cover the frying pan if you like firm yolks), about 3 minutes. Season to taste with salt and pepper. Transfer the eggs to a roasting pan and keep warm in the oven. Add a little more oil to the frying pan if necessary, and fry the remaining 4 eggs the same way.

Remove the tortillas from the oven. Using tongs, dip each tortilla quickly in the warmed tomato sauce and place on warmed individual plates. Spread ¼ cup (2 oz/60 g) of the refried beans evenly on each tortilla and top each with 2 of the fried eggs. Spoon more of the tomato sauce generously over the edges of each tortilla and the whites of the eggs, leaving the yolks uncovered. Spoon a little *crema* over the sauce, then sprinkle with the cheese and cilantro. Scatter the diced avocado, if using, around the edges of the plates and serve at once.

*Notes: Crema is a thick, rich, slightly soured type of heavy (double) cream. Queso añejo, or "aged cheese," is a mature, dry form of* queso fresco, *a soft, salty, tangy fresh cheese made from cow's milk. Panela, also a fresh cheese, is mild in flavor, with a smooth, firm, moist texture.*

MAKES 4 SERVINGS

### ROASTED TOMATO SAUCE

In a dry frying pan over high heat, roast 7 ripe, cored plum (Roma) tomatoes, turning them as they char slightly, about 5 minutes. In a food processor, combine the tomatoes; 2 or 3 serrano chiles, stemmed, seeded, and minced; ½ small white onion, chopped; and 1 large clove garlic, chopped. Process until blended but still chunky. In a large frying pan over medium-high heat, warm 1 tablespoon canola oil. Add the tomato mixture and cook, stirring constantly, until thickened, about 5 minutes. Stir in ½ teaspoon salt. Makes 1½ cups (12 fl oz/375 ml).

4 large, thick corn tortillas, preferably stale

1½ cups (12 fl oz/375 ml) **Roasted Tomato Sauce** *(far left)* or bottled salsa

¼ cup (2 fl oz/60 ml) canola oil, or as needed

8 large eggs

Fine sea salt and freshly ground pepper

1 cup (8 oz/250 g) canned refried pinto beans, warmed

⅔ cup (5 fl oz/160 ml) Mexican *crema* (see Notes), sour cream, or crème fraîche

⅓ cup (1½ oz/45 g) crumbled *queso añejo* or *panela* cheese (see Notes) or grated dry Monterey jack cheese

1 tablespoon coarsely chopped fresh cilantro (fresh coriander)

1 small avocado, halved, pitted, peeled, and cut into ½-inch (12-mm) cubes (optional)

# SHIRRED EGGS WITH SPINACH AND CRISP BREAD CRUMBS

1½ lb (750 g) spinach, well rinsed and stemmed

1 tablespoon unsalted butter

½ cup (4 fl oz/125 ml) heavy (double) cream

Fine sea salt and freshly ground pepper

Pinch of freshly grated nutmeg

4 extra-large or jumbo eggs

Crisp Bread Crumbs (far right)

Bring a large saucepan three-fourths full of lightly salted water to a boil and add the spinach. Submerge the spinach completely and cook until wilted, about 2 minutes. Immediately drain in a colander and put under cold running water until the spinach is no longer warm. Gather into balls and squeeze very firmly to extract as much water as possible. Chop coarsely.

Preheat the oven to 350°F (180°C). Generously butter an 8½-inch (21.5-cm) round gratin or similar-sized shallow baking dish.

In a large frying pan over medium heat, melt the butter. Add the spinach and cook, stirring frequently, until any excess moisture has evaporated, about 4 minutes. Stir in the cream, ½ teaspoon salt, a generous amount of pepper, and the nutmeg. Cook until thick and dry, about 2 minutes longer. Remove from the heat. Transfer the spinach to the prepared dish and smooth the top into a perfectly even surface. With the back of a large tablespoon, form 4 evenly spaced, egg-shaped pockets, 1 inch (2.5 cm) deep, in the top of the spinach. Break an egg into each depression.

Carefully transfer the dish to the oven and bake until the whites of the eggs are set and the yolks are still distinctly runny, 18–20 minutes. Scatter a few tablespoons of bread crumbs over the top of the dish and serve directly onto individual plates, scooping up the base of spinach underneath each egg.

*Note: This dish contains eggs that may be only partially cooked; for more information, see page 114.*

*Variation Tip: Prepare this dish in four ramekins, each ⅔–1 cup (5–8 fl oz/160–250 ml). Divide the spinach among them, and then break an egg into each. Cooking time will be about 10 minutes less.*

MAKES 4 SERVINGS

CRISP BREAD CRUMBS
In a small frying pan over medium-low heat, melt 2 teaspoons unsalted butter. Add ¾ cup (1½ oz/45 g) fresh sourdough bread crumbs (page 66) and 1 large clove garlic, pressed (optional). Season generously with fine sea salt and freshly ground pepper. Stir constantly until crisp and golden brown, 7–8 minutes. Remove from the heat and let cool. If desired, place in a small, airtight container and keep at room temperature for up to 24 hours before using. Makes ⅓ cup (¾ oz/20 g).

# BREAKFAST SIDES

*Planning a breakfast menu is much like selecting a dinner menu: start with a dish that wakes up the taste buds, then offer a satisfying main course. Some recipes here may be served before a substantial breakfast dish; others, alongside it. Savory sides such as crisp hash browns and salads made with the freshest fruit offer choices that will complement any breakfast menu.*

# HOME FRIES WITH RED AND GREEN BELL PEPPERS

**CHILE POWDER**

Pure ground *chile* powder is not the same as *chili* powder, which is a commercial spice blend that usually combines dried chiles, cumin, oregano, garlic, cloves, and coriander and is used to season the American Southwest stew of the same name. For the best chile flavor, seek out pure ancho chile powder, which has a good level of heat and excellent flavor. Chile powder varies in strength, and will lose its flavor over time, so purchase it in small quantities from a store with good turnover and replace it after six months.

Pour water to a depth of 1 inch (2.5 cm) into a large pot and bring to a boil. Put the whole potatoes into a collapsible steamer basket and set over the boiling water. (The boiling water should not touch the potatoes.) Cover and steam until the potatoes are tender when pierced with a small knife, 15–20 minutes, depending on their size. Transfer the potatoes to a bowl. When cool enough to handle, cut the potatoes into 1-inch (2.5-cm) cubes.

In a large cast-iron frying pan over medium-high heat, melt the butter with the oil. When the butter has foamed and the foam begins to subside, add the red and green bell peppers and the onion and cook, stirring occasionally, until the vegetables are glossy, about 5 minutes.

Add the potatoes and cook, without disturbing them, until they begin to brown, about 5 minutes. With a metal spatula, turn the potatoes over in several large portions (don't mix too much) and cook, turning (not stirring) only twice during the cooking time, to achieve the optimum crust and browning, about 15 minutes longer. Sprinkle with the chile powder, paprika, and ½ teaspoon salt and cook for 1 minute longer. Stir together to blend in the spices, then taste and adjust the seasoning. Serve at once.

*Variation Tip: Any red potato will work well in this recipe. If they are available, try tiny new potatoes. Yukon gold potatoes, with their rich, buttery flesh, are also a good choice.*

MAKES 4 SERVINGS

5 red potatoes, about 1¼ lb (625 g) total weight, scrubbed and patted dry

2 tablespoons unsalted butter

2 tablespoons canola oil

1 small red bell pepper (capsicum), seeded and cut into ¾-inch (2-cm) squares

1 small green bell pepper (capsicum), seeded and cut into ¾-inch (2-cm) squares

1 yellow onion, cut into ¾-inch (2-cm) cubes

½ teaspoon best-quality chile powder *(far left)*

½ teaspoon paprika

Fine sea salt

# LACY HASH BROWNS

2 large russet potatoes, about 1 lb (500 g) total weight, peeled, rinsed, and patted dry

2 tablespoons unsalted butter

Fine sea salt and freshly ground pepper

Just before you plan to cook the hash browns, place a clean kitchen towel on a work surface. Using the largest holes of a box grater-shredder, shred the potatoes into a mound in the center of the towel. Fold the short ends of the towel together, overlapping them, to fully enclose the potatoes. Twist the towel inward from both ends and squeeze as hard as possible to remove as much water as you can.

In a large cast-iron frying pan over medium-high heat, melt 1 tablespoon of the butter. When the butter has foamed and the foam has subsided, add the potatoes and spread them quickly into an even layer. Season with ¼ teaspoon salt and a generous grinding of pepper, and use a wide, flat spatula to press down on the potatoes firmly. Reduce the heat to medium and continue cooking, pressing down with the spatula occasionally, until the bottom is golden brown and crisp, 6–7 minutes.

Place a large plate over the top of the frying pan and hold it very securely with one hand. Using an oven mitt and a very firm grip on the handle of the frying pan with the other hand, quickly invert the potatoes onto the plate.

Add the remaining 1 tablespoon butter to the pan and return to medium-high heat. When the foam has subsided, slide the potato cake back into the pan, cooked side up. Again, season with ¼ teaspoon salt and a generous grinding of pepper. Continue cooking, pressing down with the spatula occasionally, until golden brown and crisp on the bottom, 5–6 minutes longer. Use the spatula to fold the potatoes in half and cook for 1 minute more. Transfer the hash browns to a cutting board or a platter and cut in half or into 3 wedges. Serve at once.

MAKES 2 OR 3 SERVINGS

## HASH BROWNS VARIATION

The recipe here produces a lacy, light, and thin result that is similar to the Swiss *rösti*, a crisp potato pancake. For starchier, heartier hash browns, boil the peeled potatoes in lightly salted water until just tender when pierced with the tip of a sharp knife, about 15 minutes. Drain and let cool to warm room temperature, then shred the potatoes on the largest holes of a box grater-shredder. There is no need to squeeze the cooked potato to dry; just proceed directly to frying the shredded potato as directed in the recipe.

# RED FLANNEL HASH

Bring a small saucepan three-fourths full of water to a boil over high heat. Add 1 teaspoon salt and the potatoes and simmer until the potatoes can be pierced with the tip of a sharp knife but are still quite firm, about 10 minutes. Drain and let cool, then peel and cut into ½-inch (12-mm) cubes.

Place a large cast-iron frying pan over medium heat. When it is hot, add the salt pork and sauté until crisp and browned, about 8 minutes. With a slotted spoon, transfer to a paper towel–lined plate and set aside. Remove and reserve 1 tablespoon of the fat from the pan for frying the hash. Pour off all but about 1 teaspoon of the remaining fat in the frying pan. Place the pan over medium-low heat. Add the onion and cook, stirring, until softened but not browned, about 5 minutes. Transfer the onion to a large bowl and add the potatoes, salt pork, corned beef, beets, and cream. Sprinkle with half of the parsley, ¼ teaspoon salt, and a generous grinding of pepper. Toss well, taste, and adjust the seasoning.

Return the reserved 1 tablespoon fat to the frying pan and place over medium heat. When a drop of water flicked onto the surface dances and evaporates instantly, add the potato mixture to the pan and spread it evenly. Press down with the back of a flexible metal spatula to compact and bring as much of the mixture as possible in contact with the hot pan. Reduce the heat to medium-low and cook, pressing down occasionally, until the bottom is very thick and crusty brown, about 35 minutes. Shake the pan back and forth occasionally to prevent the hash from sticking, and remove any fat that collects around the edges with a bulb baster.

Use the spatula to loosen the bottom and divide the hash into 4 portions. Scatter each portion with some of the remaining parsley and serve.

MAKES 4 SERVINGS

### HASH
Hash, a classic use for leftovers, can be anything that has been chopped and then fried, preferably in a cast-iron frying pan, which retains heat well and yields a crisp result. The only constant is potatoes. Red flannel hash takes its name from the red color that the beets give to the dish. To make standard hash, omit the beets and double the quantity of yellow onion. Any red potato will work well here, or you might try Yukon gold, a pale-skinned potato with buttery flesh.

Fine sea salt

2 or 3 large red potatoes, about 1 lb (500 g) total weight

¼ lb (125 g) lean salt pork, rind removed, cut into ¼-inch (6-mm) dice

1 small yellow onion, finely chopped

¾ lb (375 g) cooked corned beef, chopped

1 can (8¼ oz/260 g) beets, drained and chopped

¼ cup (2 fl oz/60 ml) heavy (double) cream

2 tablespoons finely chopped fresh flat-leaf (Italian) parsley

Freshly ground pepper

# POLENTINA WITH BANANAS
# AND MAPLE SYRUP

1⅔ cups (13 fl oz/410 ml) water, or more as needed

1⅔ cups (13 fl oz/410 ml) whole milk, or more as needed

1½ tablespoons sugar

Fine sea salt

¾ cup (5 oz/155 g) polenta or coarsely ground yellow cornmeal

2 ripe bananas, peeled and sliced ¼ inch (6 mm) thick

½ cup (5½ fl oz/170 ml) pure maple syrup, warmed (page 14)

Melted unsalted butter for drizzling (optional)

In a large, heavy saucepan over medium-high heat, combine the 1⅔ cups each of water and milk, sugar, and ¼ teaspoon salt and bring to a boil. Reduce the heat to very low and, when the liquid is barely simmering, drizzle in the polenta in a slow, thin stream, whisking constantly in the same direction until all the grains have been absorbed and the mixture is smooth and free of lumps. Reduce the heat to very low. Switch to a wooden spoon and stir thoroughly every 1–2 minutes until the polentina is loose and creamy, about 15 minutes. (For thicker polenta, cook for up to 30 minutes.) Add a little more water or milk if the polentina gets too stiff; this should be a very liquid mixture.

Ladle the polentina into individual bowls. Distribute the bananas over the top. Drizzle with the warm maple syrup and the melted butter, if using.

MAKES 4 SERVINGS

## POLENTA

Polenta, or cornmeal mush, can be a delicious alternative to oatmeal and shows up in many nations across the world. In Romania and Moldavia, it is known as *mamaliga*; in South Africa, as *mealie*. In 1607, English settlers who came ashore at present-day Virginia were offered steaming bowls of what the Native Americans called *rockahominy*, "corn without skin." *Polentina* refers to a creamier, more liquid form of polenta that is often served in Italy as a comforting breakfast porridge and is used as baby food.

# ROASTED TOMATOES

**FRESH BREAD CRUMBS**

To make fresh bread crumbs, use sourdough or Italian country-style bread a few days past its peak of freshness, or lay fresh bread slices flat on a countertop and leave overnight to dry out. Cut off the crusts, tear the slices into bite-sized pieces, then process in a blender or food processor to the desired texture. Store homemade bread crumbs in a zippered plastic bag in the refrigerator for up to 4 days.

Preheat the oven to 400°F (200°C). Lightly grease a small baking dish. Halve the tomatoes crosswise and scoop out the seeds and juice with a small teaspoon. Place the tomatoes, cut side up, in the prepared dish (the dish may be crowded, but the tomatoes will reduce in size as they cook). Drizzle each tomato half with a few drops of the balsamic vinegar.

Combine the bread crumbs, cheese, parsley, oil, ½ teaspoon salt, and a generous grinding of pepper in a bowl. Toss to combine. Spread the bread crumb mixture in an even layer over the cut side of each tomato half, filling up the holes left by the seeds.

Bake the tomatoes until shriveled and slightly charred around the edges, about 30 minutes. Serve warm or at room temperature.

*Notes: Do not refrigerate roasted tomatoes, or they will lose much of their flavor. If desired, push a small clove of garlic through a press and add to the bread crumbs.*

*Serving Tip: For a hearty breakfast, try serving these tomatoes along-side scrambled eggs and sausage.*

MAKES 4 SERVINGS

4 large, ripe, firm tomatoes, 6–7 oz (185–220 g) each, cored

1 teaspoon balsamic vinegar

1 cup (2 oz/60 g) fine fresh bread crumbs *(far left)*

3 tablespoons grated Parmesan cheese

2 teaspoons minced fresh flat-leaf (Italian) parsley

2 teaspoons olive oil

Fine sea salt and freshly ground pepper

# CITRUS, STRAWBERRY, AND POMEGRANATE SALAD

1 pink grapefruit, halved

1 tangerine

1½ cups (6 oz/185 g) strawberries, hulled and cut into small pieces

Seeds from 1 pomegranate *(far right)*

1 tablespoon confectioners' (icing) sugar

½ teaspoon orange flower water (see Note)

2 fresh mint sprigs for serving (optional)

Using a grapefruit knife or other small, sharp knife, loosen the grapefruit segments in each half by first carefully cutting all the way around the perimeter of each grapefruit half between the fruit and peel and then by cutting along either side of each segment to free it from its membrane. Transfer the segments to a bowl. Use scissors to snip the edges of the membranes left in each half and pull them away, leaving a clean "shell." Cut a very thin slice from the rounded ends of each grapefruit half to help it stand upright.

Cut a slice off the top and bottom of the tangerine, then stand it upright. Following the contour of the fruit, slice off the peel and white pith in thick strips. Holding the tangerine over the bowl, cut along both sides of each segment to separate it from the membrane, letting each freed segment drop into the bowl. Cut the tangerine and grapefruit segments into small pieces and return to the bowl, along with their juices.

Add the strawberries, pomegranate seeds, confectioners' sugar, and orange flower water to the bowl. Toss gently and refrigerate for 1 hour. To serve, divide the salad between the grapefruit shells. Garnish each with a mint sprig, if desired.

*Note: Orange flower water is the essence of distilled orange flowers. It is used widely in Mediterranean and Middle Eastern dishes, especially in cakes and salads. The flavor is extremely concentrated. If you use too much, this salad may taste like perfume.*

*Variation Tip: During the winter months, when fresh berries may not be available, omit the strawberries and make this recipe with 2 tangerines and 2 blood oranges.*

MAKES 2 SERVINGS

## POMEGRANATES

To seed pomegranates, working over a bowl, cut off the peel from the blossom end of the fruit, removing it with some of the white pith. Do not cut into the fruit with a knife. Instead, shallowly cut the peel into quarters, starting at the blossom end. Carefully break the fruit apart with your hands, pull back the skin, and use your fingertips to remove the seeds. If you do this in a large bowl of water, the pith will float to the surface and the seeds will sink to the bottom.

# MELON SALAD
# WITH YOGURT-HONEY DRESSING

To make the dressing, the night before, place the yogurt in a sieve lined with a double layer of damp cheesecloth (muslin) set over a bowl and refrigerate overnight.

Whisk the drained yogurt, honey, and wine together in a small bowl. Set aside.

Using a large spoon, scoop out the honeydew and cantaloupe melon flesh and cut into ¾-inch (2-cm) pieces, or scoop out with a melon baller. In a serving bowl, combine the melon pieces and the grapes and toss together gently. If desired, transfer to individual serving bowls.

Drizzle the dressing back and forth across the fruit. Scatter with the chopped pistachios and serve.

*Note: In Europe, thick and dense Greek yogurt is widely available and needs no draining. In the United States, commercial yogurt must be drained to concentrate the consistency and flavor.*

MAKES 4 SERVINGS

**FOR THE DRESSING:**

**1 cup (8 oz/250 g) plain yogurt (see Note)**

**¼ cup (3 oz/90 g) honey**

**2 tablespoons orange muscat dessert wine or other sweet, fruity wine**

**¼ small ripe honeydew melon, seeded**

**½ small ripe cantaloupe melon, seeded**

**¾ cup (4 oz/125 g) seedless green grapes, halved**

**½ cup (2 oz/60 g) coarsely chopped unsalted pistachio nuts**

## DESSERT WINE

Long enjoyed in Europe, dessert wines have gained popularity in the United States during the last decade. The most famous dessert wine, Muscat de Beaumes-de-Venise, is far too elegant to use for cooking, but would be a special treat alongside this salad. All wine-producing nations make delicious and complex sweet wines that would complement the musky melon in this recipe. If you have a bottle of another dessert wine on hand, such as Sauternes or ice wine, try it to see how it enhances the flavor of this salad.

# MORNING BREADS

*You do not have to be an experienced baker to prepare a homey coffee cake or a batch of muffins, biscuits, or scones. These quick breads allow you to fill your kitchen with the enticing aroma of freshly baked morning treats. When you have a bit more time, indulge in sweet, sticky cinnamon rolls or the famous butter-rich bread of France known as brioche.*

CRANBERRY–SOUR CREAM COFFEE CAKE
WITH STREUSEL TOPPING
74

CINNAMON ROLLS
77

BLUEBERRY MUFFINS
78

CLASSIC BAKING-POWDER BISCUITS
81

ALMOND-CURRANT SCONES
82

BANANA-RAISIN BREAD
85

BRIOCHE
86

# CRANBERRY–SOUR CREAM COFFEE CAKE WITH STREUSEL TOPPING

**STREUSEL**

Made from butter, flour, sugar, and sometimes nuts, streusel cooks into a topping similar to the American crisp and the British crumble, terms that are often used interchangeably. Streusel can be sprinkled over muffins, cupcakes, pies, or fresh, soft fruit before baking. In the oven, the butter melts and causes the dry mixture to cook into a crisp, crumbly topping. Without the butter, the mixture would simply scorch.

To make the streusel topping, in a chilled bowl, combine the butter, sugar, and flour. Using a pastry blender or 2 knives, cut the butter into the dry ingredients until the mixture is the consistency of fine, moist bread crumbs. Work the mixture with your hands until it will hold together when compressed, then squeeze it between your hands into several firm pieces. Cover and refrigerate until the cake is ready to go into the oven.

Preheat the oven to 350°F (180°C). Grease a 9-by-13-inch (23-by-33-cm) or similar-sized baking dish with butter.

Place the sour cream in a bowl and sift the baking soda and salt into it. Stir to blend evenly and set aside.

In a large bowl, using an electric mixer on medium speed or a wooden spoon, beat together the butter, sugar, and eggs until fluffy, 3–5 minutes. Sift the flour and baking powder over the top and mix in, then beat in the sour cream mixture. Scatter the chocolate chips and the drained cranberries over the top. Blend in with just a few turns of a rubber spatula. Scoop the batter into the prepared dish and smooth the surface. Scatter the streusel mixture evenly over the top, breaking it up into large crouton-sized pieces (some of the streusel mixture may be small crumbs).

Bake until a toothpick inserted into the center of the cake comes out clean but not completely dry, 40–45 minutes. Transfer to a wire rack to cool. Serve warm or at room temperature, cut into squares.

MAKES ABOUT 10 SERVINGS

FOR THE STREUSEL TOPPING:

½ cup (4 oz/125 g) cold unsalted butter, cut into 8 pieces

¼ cup (2 oz/60 g) sugar

¾ cup (4 oz/125 g) plus 2 tablespoons all-purpose (plain) flour

1¼ cups (10 oz/310 g) sour cream

1¼ teaspoons baking soda (bicarbonate of soda)

⅛ teaspoon fine sea salt

½ cup (4 oz/125 g) unsalted butter, at room temperature

1¼ cups (10 oz/315 g) sugar

2 large eggs, lightly beaten

1¾ cups (9 oz/280 g) all-purpose (plain) flour

1¾ teaspoons baking powder

½ cup (3 oz/90 g) semi-sweet (plain) chocolate chips

½ cup (2 oz/60 g) dried cranberries, soaked in warm water for 15 minutes, drained, and squeezed dry

# CINNAMON ROLLS

¼ cup (2 fl oz/60 ml) warm water (110°–115°F/43°–46°C)

½ cup (4 oz/125 g) plus 1 teaspoon granulated sugar

2½ teaspoons (1 package) active dry yeast

1 tablespoon unsalted butter, at room temperature

3½–4 cups (17½–20 oz/545–625 g) all-purpose (plain) flour

½ teaspoon fine sea salt

2 large egg yolks

1 cup (8 fl oz/250 ml) warm whole milk (110°–115°F/43°–46°C)

1½ cups (10½ oz/330 g) firmly packed light brown sugar

6 tablespoons (3 oz/90 g) unsalted butter, melted

½ cup (5 oz/155 g) light corn syrup

2 teaspoons ground cinnamon

½ cup (3 oz/90 g) raisins, soaked in warm water for 15 minutes, drained, and squeezed dry

In a bowl, combine the warm water and 1 teaspoon granulated sugar. Sprinkle with the yeast and let stand for 2 minutes, then swirl and let stand until foamy, about 5 minutes. Spread the butter over the bottom and halfway up the sides of a large bowl. In another large bowl, combine 3½ cups (17½ oz/545 g) of the flour, the ½ cup (4 oz/125 g) granulated sugar, and the salt. Make a well in the center and pour in the yeast mixture, egg yolks, and warm milk. Slowly mix together until the dough can be formed into a large ball. Transfer the dough to a floured work surface. Knead, sprinkling with the remaining flour as needed to keep the dough from sticking, until smooth and elastic, about 10 minutes. Gather into a ball, place in the buttered bowl, and turn to coat all sides. Cover with a kitchen towel. Set in a warm, draft-free place and let rise until doubled in size, about 1½ hours.

In a bowl, mix ¾ cup (6 oz/185 g) of the brown sugar, 2 tablespoons of the melted butter, and the corn syrup to a smooth paste. Scoop half into each of two 9-inch (23-cm) round cake pans and spread over the bottoms. In a small bowl, mix together the remaining brown sugar and cinnamon.

Punch down the dough. Roll into a 10-by-18-inch (25-by-45-cm) rectangle. Brush with 2 tablespoons of the melted butter. Scatter with the raisins, pressing them in lightly. Sprinkle the dough with the cinnamon-sugar mixture. Starting at one long edge, roll the dough tightly into a cylinder. Cut off and discard the rough ends. Cut the cylinder crosswise into 14 rounds. Place 1 round in the center of each pan. Arrange the remaining rounds around it. Cover and let rise until doubled, 45–60 minutes. Preheat the oven to 350°F (180°C). Brush the rolls with the remaining melted butter. Bake until golden brown, about 30 minutes. Place a wire rack over each pan and invert the rolls. Let cool and break apart to serve.

MAKES 14 ROLLS

### CINNAMON

This spice was once rare and valuable—the main reason for the Portuguese occupation of Ceylon (now Sri Lanka) in 1505 was for its superior and extensive cinnamon crop. The dried bark of a tree, cinnamon comes from two sources. The commonly available cassia cinnamon is a dark red-brown and has a strong, sweet taste. Pale tan, delicate-tasting Ceylon cinnamon is grown only in Sri Lanka and is considered by many to be true cinnamon. To grind your own, first break or crush the stick into pieces.

# BLUEBERRY MUFFINS

Preheat the oven to 400°F (200°C). Grease a standard 12-cup muffin pan, preferably nonstick.

In a large glass measuring pitcher, whisk together the eggs, brown sugar, oil, cream, milk, and vanilla.

In a large bowl, sift together the flour, baking powder, nutmeg, and salt. Make a well in the center and slowly pour in the egg mixture. Gradually mix into the dry ingredients until just combined. Add the melted butter and stir until almost smooth but still slightly lumpy. Do not overmix. The batter will be fairly thick.

Gently fold the blueberries into the muffin batter so that they are evenly distributed. Spoon the batter into the muffin cups, filling each three-fourths full. Bake until a toothpick inserted into the center of a muffin comes out clean, 20–22 minutes.

Let stand in the pan for 5 minutes, then remove each muffin from its cup with a small spatula. Serve the muffins warm, with butter, if desired.

*Note: If using frozen blueberries, leave them frozen until just before folding them into the batter. This will minimize any bleeding from the berries, which would give the muffins a gray color.*

MAKES 12 MUFFINS

### VANILLA

Vanilla beans are processed by a cold-extraction process to yield vanilla extract. Madagascar Bourbon beans are considered the best, and pure extract made from these beans carries the most intense vanilla flavor. Tahiti and Mexico also produce very good vanilla. However, some Mexican beans are known to contain coumarin, a substance that can be toxic, so purchase them only from a reputable source. While good vanilla beans can be expensive, their powerful flavor means they can be used several times: rinse them, dry completely in an airy place, and wrap airtight.

2 large eggs

½ cup (3½ oz/105 g) firmly packed dark or light brown sugar

⅓ cup (3 fl oz/80 ml) canola oil

½ cup (4 fl oz/125 ml) heavy (double) cream

½ cup (4 fl oz/125 ml) whole milk

1½ teaspoons vanilla extract (essence)

2¼ cups (11½ oz/360 g) all-purpose (plain) flour

2 teaspoons baking powder

¼ teaspoon freshly grated nutmeg

⅛ teaspoon fine sea salt

3 tablespoons unsalted butter, melted

1½ cups (6 oz/185 g) fresh or frozen blueberries (see Note)

Butter for serving (optional)

# CLASSIC BAKING-POWDER BISCUITS

2 cups (10 oz/315 g) all-purpose (plain) flour

2 teaspoons baking powder

½ teaspoon baking soda (bicarbonate of soda)

1 teaspoon fine sea salt

½ cup (4 oz/125 g) cold unsalted butter, cut into ¼-inch (6-mm) dice

⅔ cup (5 fl oz/160 ml) whole milk

Whipped butter for serving (optional)

Warmed maple syrup (page 14) for serving (optional)

Preheat the oven to 450°F (230°C). Lightly grease a baking sheet with butter.

In a large bowl, sift together the flour, baking powder, baking soda, and salt. With your fingertips, rub the cold butter into the flour until the mixture resembles coarse meal, handling it as little as possible. Stir in the milk and blend with a spoon just until all the liquid has been absorbed. With lightly floured hands, work the dough briefly *(right)* until it barely holds together in a flaky ball.

Place the dough on a lightly floured work surface. Roll or pat the dough out into a round about ½ inch (12 mm) thick. With a 2-inch (5-cm) biscuit cutter or the rim of a glass, cut out as many rounds as possible. Gather up the scraps, work into a cohesive ball, reroll, and cut out more rounds. Do not reroll the dough more than once, or you will end up with tough biscuits. Transfer the biscuits to the prepared baking sheet and bake in the center of the oven until golden brown, about 15 minutes. Serve immediately, with whipped butter and warm maple syrup, if desired.

MAKES ABOUT 9 BISCUITS

BISCUIT SAVVY

The key to making feather-light biscuits and scones (page 82) is minimal handling of the flaky, crumbly dough. You may think the dough needs more kneading to hold together, but the less you work it, the lighter the result will be. When adding the butter, work quickly so it does not melt into the dough before the biscuits go in the oven. If it becomes soft, the biscuits will be tough. Shape the dough on a lightly floured surface, gently pressing and patting it into a thick circle.

# ALMOND-CURRANT SCONES

In a food processor, combine the flour, granulated sugar, baking powder, baking soda, and salt. Pulse twice to blend. Add the butter and orange zest and pulse 3 or 4 times until the mixture looks like large bread crumbs. Transfer to a large bowl.

In a large glass measuring pitcher, whisk together the eggs and the buttermilk. Pour over the dry ingredients and scatter in the almonds and currants. Stir only until the mixture is evenly blended and comes together into a soft dough. Using a light touch, form the dough into 10 large, flattened rounds (each about the size of a tennis ball) or 16 medium, flattened rounds (each about the size of a golfball). Place 1 inch (2.5 cm) apart on 1 large or 2 small ungreased baking sheets. Place in the refrigerator to chill for at least 15 minutes or for up to overnight (cover with plastic wrap if refrigerating overnight).

Preheat the oven to 375°F (190°C). Sprinkle a pinch of the raw sugar on top of each scone. Bake until pale golden brown on top, about 20 minutes. Let cool briefly on a rack, then serve at once.

MAKES 10 LARGE OR 16 MEDIUM SCONES

## DRIED FRUITS

Currants are a traditional ingredient in scones, a classic British treat often served at breakfast and tea and similar to what Americans call biscuits. Unlike the tart fresh currants used to make jellies and jams, tiny dried currants are actually dried Zante grapes, or raisins. You can use other dried fruits in place of the currants, including cherries, cranberries, blueberries, or finely chopped apricots. The sweetness and chewy texture that dried fruits impart are the perfect counterpoint to the crunchy almonds in these scones.

4 cups (1½ lb/625 g) all-purpose (plain) flour

3 tablespoons granulated sugar

2 teaspoons baking powder

1 teaspoon baking soda (bicarbonate of soda)

¼ teaspoon fine sea salt

1 cup (8 oz/250 g) cold unsalted butter, cut into 16 cubes

Grated zest of 1 orange

2 large eggs

1 cup (8 fl oz/250 ml) plus 2 tablespoons buttermilk

¾ cup (2½ oz/75 g) slivered blanched almonds

¾ cup (4½ oz/140 g) dried currants

2 tablespoons raw or turbinado sugar

# BANANA-RAISIN BREAD

2 cups (10 oz/315 g) all-purpose (plain) flour

¾ cup (6 oz/185 g) sugar

¾ teaspoon baking soda (bicarbonate of soda)

½ teaspoon fine sea salt

1¼ cups (7½ oz/235 g) golden raisins (sultanas), currants, and/or standard raisins

3 very ripe bananas, peeled and mashed (about 1½ cups/9 oz/280 g)

¼ cup (2 oz/60 g) plain yogurt or ¼ cup (2 fl oz/60 ml) buttermilk

2 large eggs, lightly beaten

⅓ cup (3 fl oz/80 ml) canola oil

1 teaspoon vanilla extract (essence)

Grease and flour a 9-by-5-inch (23-by-13-cm) loaf pan, preferably nonstick. Place a rack in the lower third of the oven and preheat to 350°F (180°C).

In a large bowl, combine the flour, sugar, baking soda, salt, and raisins and toss to mix thoroughly.

In another bowl, use a wooden spoon to mix together the bananas, yogurt, eggs, oil, and vanilla. With a rubber spatula, fold the banana mixture into the dry ingredients until just combined and quite chunky. Scoop the batter into the prepared pan.

Bake until the bread is firm and golden brown, and a toothpick inserted into the center comes out clean, about 1 hour. Let cool in the pan for 5 minutes, then turn out onto a rack. Serve warm or at room temperature.

*Note: This bread will keep, tightly wrapped and refrigerated, for up to 1 week. Bring to room temperature before slicing.*

*Variation Tip: To make Banana-Rum-Raisin Bread, soak the raisins in 3 tablespoons warmed dark or spiced rum for 25 minutes, tossing occasionally. Add the soaked raisins and any rum remaining in the bowl to the banana mixture before folding the wet and dry ingredients together.*

MAKES ONE 9-BY-5-INCH (23-BY-13-CM) LOAF

BANANAS FOR BAKING

Unlike vegetables, some fruits improve in taste and texture after they are picked and allowed to age a bit. This is particularly true of the banana, which, like the avocado (also a fruit), is virtually inedible in its underripe state. Bananas are at their sweetest and most delicious when overripe and mushy, the perfect condition for making this flavorful bread recipe.

# BRIOCHE

**BRIOCHE DOUGH**

Brioche is one of the most
venerable breads in France's
rich culinary heritage. This
butter-laden bread is light,
airy, and so rich that it
seems more like a cake than
a bread. Making brioche
requires a cool and confident
hand: cool because if your
hands are too hot, the butter
can seep out of the dough,
and confident because the
dough may appear at first as
if it is too soft to work. Using
a floured dough scraper
solves both problems, though
you may have to scrape the
scraper to return any errant
scraps of wet dough to the
main mass.

Cut the butter into 24 small cubes and place on a plate in the freezer for 20 minutes.

Place the warm milk in a large measuring pitcher, sprinkle the yeast and 1 teaspoon of the sugar over the top, and let stand for 2 minutes. Swirl to combine and let stand until foamy, about 5 minutes longer. Whisk the eggs into the yeast mixture.

In a large food processor, preferably fitted with the plastic dough blade (the metal blade will also work), combine the flour, salt, and remaining 2 teaspoons sugar. Add the frozen butter to the processor and pulse 15–20 times in 2-second bursts to break the butter up into flour-covered "pebbles." With the motor running, add the liquid ingredients to the butter-flour mixture and keep processing until the dough comes together into a rough mass on the center column, about 15 seconds. If necessary, add milk a few drops at a time until the dough is wet enough to form a soft and slightly sticky mass. The dough will be more like a paste than regular bread dough.

Let the dough stand in the processor for 5 minutes, then process for 30 seconds longer. Using a plastic spatula, scrape the dough out onto a lightly floured board and let rest for 2 minutes. With a floured, flexible dough scraper (not your hands), knead 25 times, then transfer to a lightly oiled bowl. Cover with plastic wrap and refrigerate overnight. The dough will rise only slightly.

Thoroughly grease and flour 6 fluted brioche molds 3–4 inches (7.5–10 cm) in diameter. Remove the dough from the refrigerator and be prepared to begin shaping the dough at once, while it is still very cold. Lightly flour your hands and a work surface. Divide the dough into 6 equal pieces and shape each into a ball.

1 cup (8 oz/250 g)
unsalted butter

1½ tablespoons warm
whole milk (110°–115°F/
43°–46°C), or more as
needed

1 teaspoon active dry
yeast

3 teaspoons sugar

3 large eggs, lightly beaten

1¾ cups (9 oz/280 g)
all-purpose (plain) flour

1 teaspoon fine sea salt

**FOR THE GLAZE:**

**1 large egg**

**2 tablespoons whole milk**

Working with 1 ball at a time, use the side of your hand to pinch apart about one-third of the dough *without* going all the way through. Roll back and forth against the "neck" of the dough to create a small "head." Place the dough piece, head side up, into a prepared mold. Press the base of the neck down into the larger ball in 2 or 3 places to anchor it, without twisting. This will prevent the head from rising so far that it flops over during rising and baking. Repeat to shape the remaining brioches.

Place the filled molds on a baking sheet and cover loosely with a tent of aluminum foil; do not let the foil touch the dough. Let rise again for about 1 hour. The dough will increase in size slightly but will not double.

Preheat the oven to 375°F (190°C) and place 2 racks in the lowest 2 oven positions. Five minutes before you put the brioches in the oven, place a small roasting pan containing ½ inch (12 mm) boiling water on the lowest rack.

To make the glaze, beat the egg and milk together. Brush the brioches gently with the glaze and place on the upper rack. Immediately increase the oven temperature to 400°F (200°C) and bake until golden brown and firm, about 18 minutes. Let stand for 1 minute, then remove from the molds and let cool briefly on a rack. Serve warm.

MAKES 6 BRIOCHES

*(Photograph appears on following page.)*

**BRIOCHE MOLDS**

Believed to have first been used sometime during the early 1900s, brioche molds are narrow at the bottom and wide at the top and have attractively fluted sides. As the breads bake, they are imprinted with this fluted design at their base and rise and expand above the edge of the molds to form an impressive broad cap. Brioche molds are usually made from tinned steel; some have nonstick interiors. They come in many sizes and are often described by the number of flutes they contain.

# WEEKEND BRUNCH

*Breakfast's more formal cousin should gratify more than a passing hunger: It should keep you and your guests satisfied until dinnertime. A weekend brunch dish, whether a soufflé, a strata, or a quiche, tends to be more refined and sophisticated than its weekday counterpart. For such an occasion, consider offering a choice of special beverages (see page 113).*

# CHERRY-CHEESE BLINTZES

To make the blintzes, in a blender, combine the eggs, milk, flour, salt, and 2 tablespoons melted butter. Blend for 10 seconds, then scrape down the sides and blend for 20 seconds longer. Place a 6-inch (15-cm) crepe pan or a small nonstick frying pan over medium heat and brush with a thin film of melted butter. Use a ladle to quickly pour in 2 tablespoons of the batter. Swirl the pan to coat the bottom with the batter. Cook until the bottom is golden and the top is just set, about 45 seconds. With a nonstick spatula, transfer the blintz to a plate, browned side down; do not cook the other side. Repeat with the remaining batter, brushing the pan with more butter between each blintz.

To make the filling, in a large bowl, whisk the cream cheese, farmer's cheese, sugar, egg, lemon juice, vanilla, and cinnamon with a fork until smooth. Stir in the cherries.

To assemble the blintzes, line a platter with parchment (baking) paper. Place each blintz in front of you, browned side up, and place 2 generous tablespoons of filling in the center. Fold the 2 outer edges toward the center so they meet over the filling. Pat gently to flatten. Fold the top and bottom in to overlap slightly in the center. Place, seam side down, on the platter. If not cooking immediately, cover and refrigerate for up to 8 hours (bring back to room temperature for 10 minutes before cooking).

To cook the blintzes, place a large frying pan over medium-low heat and add 1 tablespoon of the butter. When the butter foams, add 4 or 5 blintzes, seam side down; do not crowd the pan. Sauté until golden, about 5 minutes. Turn and cook until golden, about 3 minutes. Keep warm in a low (200°F / 95°C) oven, loosely covered with aluminum foil. Arrange 2 or 3 warm blintzes on each plate. Top with a dollop of jelly and serve.

MAKES ABOUT 22 BLINTZES

## CHERRIES

Cherries fall into two main categories: sweet and tart. The most common sweet varieties are the light-colored Royal Ann and the widely grown deep red Bing. Tart varieties include Montmorency (rare in Europe but widespread in the United States) and the darker Morello. Any sweet or canned tart cherry would be appropriate in this recipe. If you prefer to use fresh sweet cherries, pit them with a cherry pitter or a small, sharp knife. Make sure they are very ripe, or poach them for 5 minutes in sweetened water. Tart cherries are rarely sold fresh.

FOR THE BLINTZES:

4 large eggs

1 cup (8 fl oz/250 ml) whole milk

1 cup (5 oz/155 g) all-purpose (plain) flour

⅛ teaspoon fine sea salt

2 tablespoons unsalted butter, melted, plus extra for cooking

FOR THE FILLING:

½ lb (250 g) cream cheese, at room temperature

½ lb (250 g) farmer's cheese (page 114)

¼ cup (2 oz/60 g) sugar

1 large egg

1 teaspoon lemon juice

½ teaspoon vanilla extract (essence)

¼ teaspoon ground cinnamon

1 cup (6 oz/185 g) jarred sweet or tart cherries, drained and halved, or pitted fresh cherries

4–5 tablespoons unsalted butter

Fruit jelly or preserves such as apricot

# WILD MUSHROOM QUICHE

Cheese Pastry *(far right)*, rolled out into a 10-by-14-inch (25-by-35-cm) rectangle or 13-inch (33-cm) round

1¾ cups (14 fl oz/430 ml) whole milk

1 oz (30 g) dried porcino mushrooms

3 tablespoons unsalted butter

3 tablespoons olive oil

3 shallots, finely chopped

¾ lb (375 g) mixed fresh wild and cultivated mushrooms such as chanterelle, shiitake, and cremini, stems trimmed, brushed clean, and sliced

3 large leeks, white parts only, thinly sliced

1½ tablespoons chopped fresh tarragon

Fine sea salt and freshly ground pepper

1 tablespoon Dijon mustard

¾ cup (6 fl oz/180 ml) heavy (double) cream

3 large whole eggs plus 2 large egg yolks, at room temperature

Transfer the pastry to a 9-by-13-inch (23-by-33-cm) tart pan with 2-inch (5-cm) removable sides or a 12-inch (30-cm) round tart pan with removable sides. Ease the pastry into the pan and fold any overhanging pastry back over itself, pressing it into the sides to extend slightly above the rim. Prick with a fork and refrigerate for 30 minutes. Preheat the oven to 400°F (200°C). Line the shell with parchment (baking) paper and fill with ceramic pie weights. Bake until the edges begin to shrink away from the pan, about 15 minutes. Remove the paper and weights and bake until the bottom appears dry, about 4 minutes longer. Let cool on a wire rack.

Reduce the oven temperature to 375°F (190°C). In a saucepan over medium heat, warm the milk to just below the boiling point. Remove from the heat, add the dried porcini, and swirl to cover. Let stand until softened, 20–30 minutes. Squeeze the mushrooms, draining the milk back into the pan. Chop the porcini and strain the milk through a fine-mesh sieve. Set both aside separately.

Meanwhile, in a sauté pan over medium-high heat, melt 2 tablespoons each of the butter and olive oil. Reduce the heat to medium and sauté the shallots, stirring, until softened, about 3 minutes. Add all the mushrooms and sauté, stirring, until tender and no liquid remains, about 8 minutes. Transfer to a bowl. In the same pan over low heat, melt the remaining butter and olive oil. Add the leeks and cook, covered, until tender, about 12 minutes. Add the tarragon, season with salt and pepper, and cook for 1 minute.

Spread the base of the pastry shell evenly with the mustard and then the mushroom and leek mixtures. In a bowl, whisk together the reserved milk, cream, eggs and egg yolks, ½ teaspoon salt, and ¼ teaspoon pepper. Pour over the vegetables. Bake the quiche until all but the very center is set and lightly browned, 25–30 minutes. Let cool on a rack for 15 minutes. Cut into squares and serve.

MAKES 6–8 SERVINGS

### CHEESE PASTRY

In a food processor, pulse ¼ lb (125 g) diced Gruyère cheese. Add 1½ cups (7½ oz/235 g) all-purpose (plain) flour and ¼ teaspoon salt and pulse until finely crumbled. Add ½ cup (4 oz/125 g) chilled unsalted butter cut into pieces and pulse until it resembles fluffy bread crumbs. Lightly beat 1 egg, drizzle over the mixture, and pulse twice. Scrape down the bowl sides. Sprinkle 2 tablespoons cold water over the mixture and pulse until a rough mass forms, adding another tablespoon of water if needed. Refrigerate for at least 2 hours. Let sit at room temperature for 20 minutes before using.

# GOAT CHEESE AND SPANISH HAM SOUFFLÉ

Preheat the oven to 400°F (200°C). Place a baking sheet on the bottom rack. Generously grease a sturdy 9-inch (23-cm) round or 7-by-10-inch (18-by-25-cm) oval gratin dish or a 6-cup (48–fl oz/ 1.5-l) soufflé dish and place in the freezer.

In a small saucepan over medium heat, melt the butter. When the foam has subsided, whisk in the flour. Cook, stirring constantly, until the mixture is bubbling and has only just begun to brown, about 2 minutes. Slowly drizzle in the milk, whisking constantly to prevent lumps from forming. Simmer, stirring occasionally, until the mixture thickens, about 5 minutes. Remove from the heat. Stir in ¼ teaspoon salt and a generous grinding of pepper. Quickly whisk in the egg yolks until completely blended.

In a large, spotlessly clean bowl, combine the egg whites and a large pinch of salt. Using a mixer on high speed, beat almost until stiff peaks form when the beaters are lifted. Thoroughly stir about one-third of the yolk mixture into the egg whites, then using a large rubber spatula, fold in the remaining yolk mixture, taking care not to crush too much air out of the egg whites. Crumble the goat cheese over the mixture in pea-sized pieces, and scatter the ham and parsley over the top. Fold the mixture once or twice to distribute the ingredients; do not overmix. Scoop the mixture into the prepared dish, smooth the top gently, and place in the oven.

Bake until puffed and golden and still a little bit wobbly in the center, about 25 minutes. Serve at once.

*Note: Spanish serrano ham is salted and hung in drying halls to air-cure. It is similar to its more famous Italian cousin, prosciutto, but is traditionally cut thicker and has a more earthy flavor.*

MAKES 4 SERVINGS

1½ tablespoons unsalted butter

1½ tablespoons all-purpose (plain) flour

1 cup (8 fl oz/250 ml) whole milk

Fine sea salt and freshly ground pepper

5 large eggs, separated

5 oz (155 g) very cold fresh goat cheese

¾ cup (3 oz/90 g) finely diced serrano ham (see Note) or prosciutto

1 tablespoon chopped fresh flat-leaf (Italian) parsley

# FOCACCIA WITH SMOKED SALMON AND CRÈME FRAÎCHE

FOR THE DOUGH:

3½ cups (17½ oz/545 g) all-purpose (plain) flour

2½ teaspoons (1 package) active dry yeast

1 tablespoon sugar

1 teaspoon fine sea salt

1¼ cups (10 fl oz/310 ml) warm water (110°–115°F/ 43°–46°C)

2 tablespoons olive oil

Olive oil for brushing

Fine sea salt and freshly ground pepper

1 cup (8 oz/250 g) crème fraîche *(far right)* or mascarpone cheese

6 oz (185 g) sliced smoked salmon, coarsely chopped

½ small red onion, halved lengthwise, then slivered lengthwise

4 green (spring) onions, including tender green parts, thinly sliced

¼ cup (2 oz/60 g) capers, rinsed and drained

2 oz (60 g) salmon roe caviar (optional)

To make the dough, in a food processor, combine the flour, yeast, sugar, and salt and pulse to blend. With the motor running, add the warm water and olive oil in a steady stream, and pulse until the dough comes together in a rough mass. Process for about 40 seconds longer, then knead into a smooth, soft ball on a floured work surface. Place the dough in a large, oiled bowl and turn to coat on all sides. Cover with plastic wrap, set in a warm, draft-free place, and let the dough rise until doubled in size, about 1½ hours. Punch down the dough and divide into 2 equal pieces. Shape each piece into a disk and dust with flour. Wrap tightly in plastic wrap and refrigerate for at least 1 hour or for up to 3 hours.

Preheat the oven to 500°F (260°C). Remove the dough from the refrigerator. Place on a floured work surface. Form each disk into a ball, cover with a kitchen towel, and let rest for 10 minutes. Place each ball in the center of a lightly oiled, large rimless baking sheet and roll out into a rough oval shape about ⅜ inch (1 cm) thick. (If the dough resists, cover with a kitchen towel, let rest for 3–4 minutes, and roll again.) Cover with a kitchen towel and let stand for at least 20 minutes or for up to 40 minutes.

Brush the dough lightly with olive oil and season generously with salt and pepper. Bake until crisp and slightly golden, about 15 minutes. Check after 5 minutes and poke any rising air bubbles with a knife. Transfer to a cutting board or large platter. Spread the warm focaccia with the crème fraîche. Scatter the smoked salmon, red onion, green onions, capers, and salmon roe, if using, over the top. Use a large knife to slice into wedges.

*Note: The dough can be frozen for up to 1 month in a zippered plastic bag. Let it thaw overnight in the refrigerator.*

MAKES 4 SERVINGS

## CRÈME FRAÎCHE

A soured cultured cream product originally from France, crème fraîche is similar to sour cream but sweeter. To make your own, combine 1 cup (8 fl oz/250 ml) heavy (double) cream and 1 tablespoon buttermilk in a saucepan over medium-low heat. Heat to lukewarm; do not allow to simmer. Remove from the heat, cover, and allow to thicken at warm room temperature, from 8 to 48 hours. Once it is as thick and flavorful as you like, refrigerate to chill it before using.

# PEPPER JACK AND JALAPEÑO SPOONBREAD

Preheat the oven to 350°F (180°C). Generously grease a 10-inch (25-cm) round or 8-by-10-inch (20-by-25-cm) oval baking dish or cast-iron frying pan.

In a bowl, whisk together the cornmeal and 1 cup (8 fl oz/250 ml) of the milk. In a large saucepan over medium-high heat, heat the remaining 2 cups (16 fl oz/500 ml) milk until small bubbles appear along the edges of the pan. Pour the cornmeal-milk mixture into the pan and bring to a simmer, stirring constantly. Cook until the cornmeal has thickened enough to see the bottom of the pan when you stir, about 5 minutes. Remove from the heat and stir in the jalapeño(s), cilantro, cheese, egg yolks, sugar, and salt.

In a spotlessly clean bowl, using an electric mixer on high speed, beat the egg whites until stiff peaks form when the beaters are lifted. Stir one-fourth of the egg whites thoroughly into the cornmeal mixture to lighten it, then fold in the remaining whites, being careful not to overmix. Pour into the prepared dish.

Bake until puffed and golden, and a toothpick inserted in the center comes out clean, about 45 minutes. Serve at once, sprinkling the green onion and a little hot sauce, if using, over each serving.

MAKES 4–6 SERVINGS

## HANDLING CHILES

To reduce some of the heat in hot chiles, such as the jalapeños used in this recipe, cut out the membranes, or ribs, and discard the seeds. This is where the capsaicin, the hot element of a chile, is concentrated. If you like heat, leave in a few seeds. When handling chiles, avoid touching sensitive areas such as your eyes or mouth. When finished, wash your hands, the cutting board, and the knife thoroughly with hot, soapy water.

1 cup (5 oz/155 g) yellow cornmeal

3 cups (24 fl oz/750 ml) whole milk

1 or 2 large jalapeño chiles, seeded and minced

1 tablespoon finely chopped fresh cilantro (fresh coriander)

½ lb (250 g) pepper jack, Sonoma jack, Monterey jack, or Havarti cheese, cut into ½-inch (12-mm) cubes

4 large eggs, separated (page 96), at room temperature

Pinch of sugar

1 teaspoon fine sea salt

2 tablespoons thinly sliced green onion, tender green parts only

Hot-pepper sauce for serving (optional)

# BROCCOLI RABE, PESTO, AND SMOKED MOZZARELLA STRATA

¾ lb (375 g) broccoli rabe, thick stems removed

5 slices sourdough bread, about ½ inch (12 mm) thick, crusts removed

¼ cup (2 fl oz/60 ml) pesto (page 112)

1½ cups (6 oz/185 g) shredded smoked mozzarella cheese

1 cup (8 fl oz/250 ml) whole milk

¾ cup (6 fl oz/180 ml) heavy (double) cream

4 large eggs

2 teaspoons Dijon mustard

Fine sea salt and freshly ground pepper

Bring a large saucepan of lightly salted water to a boil. Add the broccoli rabe and blanch until almost tender, about 5 minutes. Drain immediately and rinse under cold running water until cool throughout. Gather into a ball and squeeze out as much water as possible. Chop the broccoli rabe coarsely.

Generously grease a 7-by-11-inch (18-by-28-cm) or similar-sized baking dish, and place about 2½ slices of the bread in the base, cutting as necessary to make an even layer. Spread the broccoli rabe evenly over the bread. Add the pesto in dollops, spacing them evenly. Scatter with half of the smoked mozzarella and top with the remaining bread, again cutting to fit.

In a large bowl, combine the milk, cream, eggs, mustard, ½ teaspoon salt, and a generous grinding of pepper. Whisk vigorously until smooth. Pour the custard mixture over the bread and use the back of a large, flat spoon to press the bread down into the custard mixture. Cover the baking dish with plastic wrap and let stand at room temperature for 30 minutes. Meanwhile, preheat the oven to 350°F (180°C). Press the bread down into the custard after about 15 minutes, and again just before placing in the oven.

Sprinkle the top with the remaining cheese. Bake until puffed, golden, and crisp, about 45 minutes. Let stand for 5 minutes, then cut into squares and serve.

MAKES 4–6 SERVINGS

## BROCCOLI RABE

Related to broccoli, cabbage, and mustard, this cruciferous vegetable has slender stalks with small, jagged leaves and florets that resemble tiny heads of broccoli. Broccoli rabe has a mild, pleasantly bitter taste with overtones of sweet mustard. Before using broccoli rabe, remove any wilted leaves and trim any tough stem ends. Blanching reduces some of the bitterness. Broccoli raab, rape, *rapini*, and Italian broccoli are other names by which this vegetable is known.

# PRUNE AND ARMAGNAC CLAFOUTIS

In a bowl, combine the prunes, Armagnac, and hot water. Toss to combine. Let stand at room temperature, tossing occasionally, until the prunes are plump, about 30 minutes.

Preheat the oven to 400°F (200°C). Grease the bottom and sides of a 9-inch (23-cm) oval or similar-sized baking dish and flour the inside, shaking out the excess.

In a bowl, whisk the whole egg and egg yolk together, then whisk in the granulated sugar. Add the flour and stir to combine. Whisk in the cream and melted butter. With a slotted spoon, transfer the prunes to the base of the prepared dish. Whisk the remaining soaking liquid into the egg batter and pour the batter evenly over the prunes.

Bake until puffy and golden, about 30 minutes. Serve directly from the dish, or let cool slightly, invert onto a rack, and turn right side up onto a serving platter. Serve warm, dusted with a little confectioners' sugar.

MAKES 4 SERVINGS

2 cups (12 oz/375 g) pitted prunes, halved

3 tablespoons Armagnac or Cognac

3 tablespoons very hot water (120°F/49°C)

1 large whole egg plus 1 large egg yolk

⅓ cup (3 oz/90 g) granulated sugar

3 tablespoons all-purpose (plain) flour

1 cup (8 fl oz/250 ml) heavy (double) cream

3 tablespoons unsalted butter, melted

Confectioners' (icing) sugar for serving

# BREAKFAST BASICS

*In the morning, we all need fuel to function. A good night's sleep and a cup of coffee are simply not enough to prepare us for a busy day. Physicians and nutritionists agree: Starting the day with a balanced breakfast is the best favor you can do for your body. And, just because breakfast is good for you doesn't mean it has to be boring. As the recipes in this book demonstrate, spices, herbs, fresh and dried fruits, and vegetables all can enliven breakfast standards, turning them into delicious morning meals.*

## EQUIPMENT

When making breakfast, whether you are cooking eggs, hash browns, or waffles, it is important to use the right pan or other cookware to ensure optimum results.

### CAST IRON

When you want to sear food until golden brown and beautifully crusty, the surface of choice is well-seasoned cast iron. Cast iron heats more slowly than some other materials, but it holds the heat extremely well and uniformly over a pan's surface.

Cast iron is a great choice for cooking foods such as hash browns and home fries as well as sausages, bacon, and other meats. It is a less desirable option for cooking foods that contain acidic ingredients such as lemon juice, tomatoes, or vinegar; cast iron can react with these ingredients and impart a metallic taste. Be aware, as well, that eggs scrambled in a cast-iron pan may acquire a harmless greenish tint.

Great importance has always been placed on the proper care of cast-iron cookware, especially seasoning. The process of seasoning a cast-iron pan keeps it from rusting and prevents foods from sticking. To season a pan before its first use, heat it over high heat, coat it with vegetable oil, and use paper towels to spread the oil and rub it into the metal, which will eventually blacken. Repeat this procedure when the coating starts to wear away and rust begins to appear. Failure to season a cast-iron pan properly can result in exposure to heavy metals (lead), which would make it unsafe for food use.

### NONSTICK

When nonstick cookware debuted some years ago, the quality was poor, and the coating tended to chip and scratch easily, causing serious cooks to shun the new option. Since then, the technology has advanced, and acquiring a good-quality nonstick frying pan is essential for every home cook. Even professional chefs are using and praising this formerly maligned cookware.

Frying pans and sauté pans are the best choices for nonstick pans. Sometimes called a skillet, a frying pan is broad with sides that often slightly flare outward. A sauté pan has relatively high, straight sides, which help to keep the heat in the pan so the food cooks quickly. In either case, purchase pans that are heavy and have an ovenproof handle. You will want small (8-inch/20-cm), medium (10-inch/25-cm), and large (12-inch/30-cm) pans for the most versatility. If you make omelets often, you may want to invest in a nonstick omelet pan, which is similar to a frying pan but has shallow, sloping sides and a long handle. These features make it ideal for cooking and folding omelets.

Keep in mind that although a nonstick pan is ideal for making omelets, pancakes, and oatmeal, its coated surface will interfere with browning meat.

When cooking in a nonstick pan, be sure to use wooden or heatproof plastic or rubber utensils. Those made from metal may scratch the nonstick surface. Wash nonstick pans by hand to preserve their finish.

## OTHER COOKWARE

Stainless steel or hard-anodized aluminum pans also work well for browning foods, but starchy foods, such as potatoes, may stick to them. However, unlike cast iron, these materials will not react with acidic ingredients.

## WAFFLE IRONS

It is hard to imagine today, but until recently waffle irons were made of uncoated metal, and the chances of serving a waffle that was completely intact were slim. With the advent of nonstick waffle irons, preparing perfect waffles is much easier. If you have an older waffle iron or prefer one with an uncoated surface, make sure you season it according to the manufacturer's instructions. Seasoned or nonstick irons do not need greasing and are not washed. Simply brush out any crumbs after use. Waffle irons are available in several shapes, such as circles, squares, and hearts. Some are heated on the stove top; many are electric.

# PANCAKES AND WAFFLES

Batters for pancakes, waffles, and crepes are similar to those for cakes, popovers, and Yorkshire puddings in that they are all thin mixtures of flour, liquid, and usually butter. Different proportions change the final result, as does the addition of eggs, yeast, or baking powder and/or baking soda (bicarbonate of soda) for leavening power.

The batters for most waffles and pancakes use baking powder and/or baking soda. For some recipes, such as Belgian Waffles (page 26), the batter should stand before cooking, which allows the starch molecules in the flour to swell. Other recipes, such as Swedish Pancake (page 34), have one of the simplest batters, using only lightly beaten whole eggs for rising power.

For the most tender results, use a light hand when mixing pancake and waffle batter, so the gluten in the flour does not overdevelop.

## PANCAKES

For making pancakes, a nonstick griddle or a heavy nonstick frying pan is indispensable. Griddles, flat round or rectangular pans, are designed to sit flat on the stove top over one or two burners. Begin by preheating the pan until a drop of water flicked onto the surface dances and evaporates instantly. Then brush with a little melted butter and ladle out the batter. The pancakes are ready to turn when the edges appear dry and the surfaces are covered with bubbles.

Cook the pancakes in batches, depending on the size of your pan or griddle, and transfer them to a low (200°F/95°C) oven to keep warm before serving.

## WAFFLES

When making waffles, be sure to preheat the waffle iron. Then pour on the batter, evenly covering only about two-thirds of the grid surface, to leave room for the waffle to rise. If you overfill the grid, the excess batter will bubble out of the waffle iron.

Do not be tempted to open the waffle iron during cooking; checking the waffle before it is ready will result in a split, ragged waffle. Instead, follow the manufacturer's instructions, and also rely on your sense of smell to determine doneness. The waffle is cooked properly shortly after it begins to smell toasty, when all steam has stopped emerging from the iron, and the top of the iron lifts away without resistance. As for pancakes, cook waffles in batches, and transfer them to a low (200°F/95°C) oven to keep warm before serving.

## BREAKFAST BREADS

Two main types of breads are typically made for breakfast: quick breads, such as coffee cakes, muffins, biscuits, and scones, and more time-consuming yeast breads, such as brioche and cinnamon rolls.

Quick breads are prepared with chemical leaveners, such as baking powder or baking soda. Baking powder is a mixture of an acid and an alkaline, or base, that is activated when it is exposed to moisture or heat. When activated, it releases carbon dioxide gas, which in turn leavens a batter, causing it to rise as it cooks. Baking soda is an alkaline, or base, that releases carbon dioxide gas only when it comes into contact with an acidic ingredient, such as sour cream, yogurt, buttermilk, or citrus juice. The leavening effect of baking powder or soda will wear off if a quick-bread batter is not exposed to heat, so bake the batters as soon as possible after mixing.

Quick breads do not have the complex flavor achieved by using yeast and allowing the dough to rise before baking, but they make up for this by incorporating spices, fresh or dried fruit, and nuts. If you lack time to prepare a yeast bread, a quick bread offers a versatile, efficient, and delicious alternative.

The first step in making a yeast bread is activating the yeast: mixed into warm liquid, the yeast begins, within 5 to 10 minutes, to bubble into a thick foam. Professional bakers refer to this procedure as "proofing" the yeast, or testing it to make sure it is still active. If no bubbling occurs, discard the yeast and purchase new yeast. When yeast is proofed, it also gets a head start on multiplying before it is added to the other ingredients.

Yeast breads also require time for kneading and rising. The folding and pressing of a yeast dough that happens during kneading allows it to develop the strands of gluten that, when baked, will stretch out and form pockets of air, thus inflating the dough and yielding a light and airy texture. Without kneading, the result would be a heavy, bricklike loaf.

Allowing the dough to rise stretches the gluten and brings out the flavor; the longer the dough rises, the more flavor the bread will have. Yeast has only a finite amount of rising power, however. The key is to meet but not exceed that power by keeping the dough at a moist, warm temperature, and not exceeding the recommended rising time. Otherwise, the yeast will lose its potency and the bread will be heavy and dense.

## FRESH FRUIT

Morning is the perfect time for enjoying the sweet, refreshing taste of fruit, whether in the form of a salad or compote or a glass of fresh juice. Here are some tips for purchasing some of the most common fruit varieties served at breakfast and used for juicing citrus.

When ripe, melons such as honeydew and cantaloupe should yield just slightly at the blossom end; most important, they should have an appealing, sweet perfume. Citrus fruits in their prime should feel heavy for their size and give off a pleasant citrusy aroma at the blossom end. Cherries and berries are best only when ripe and in season. Ready-to-eat apricots and peaches should yield slightly when gently pressed. If not quite ripe, set them out at room temperature for a day or two.

A citrus reamer works well for making a single glass of juice. To produce fresh juice in large quantities, you will want to purchase an electric juicer or a citrus attachment for a food processor or stand mixer. Look for an attachment that accommodates different-sized reamers. A reamer that works efficiently for making orange juice is far too small to juice grapefruit. Juice presses with levered handles will also work well.

# EGGS

Nutritionally balanced, inexpensive, incredibly versatile, and delicious—the egg is a valued breakfast staple. Legend has it that each pleat on a chef's toque represents another way that eggs may be prepared.

## SIZES AND GRADES

Applied to eggs, the term *quality* refers to freshness rather than nutrition. The highest-quality eggs, designated at the time of packing, are grade AA, which have thick whites and firm, plump yolks. Grade A eggs follow closely behind, but grade B eggs, low in quality, seldom reach the retail market. Eggs are also labeled by size: jumbo, extra-large, large, medium, small, and peewee. Most recipes use large eggs, and although other sizes may be substituted, you might have to adjust the recipe.

Free-range eggs come from hens that are, in theory, free to forage, scratch, and dig as nature intended. As a result, the hens pick up added nutrients unavailable to chickens that are caged. Free-range eggs are gathered by hand, and the hens receive no animal cholesterol in their diets. These eggs tend to be richer in flavor and have a yellower yolk.

When purchasing eggs from either free-range or caged chickens, choose large AA eggs if possible. Make sure that the eggs are not cracked and that their shells are clean. Also check the sell-by date, and avoid eggs that are nearing this cutoff.

## STORAGE

Once eggs have been brought home from the market, store them in a cold area of the refrigerator, where the temperature is below 40°F (4°C). Do not leave eggs at room temperature; eggs set out for a day on a countertop age as much as they would during a full week in the refrigerator. Also avoid storing them on the egg racks found in some refrigerator doors; the eggs may not stay cold enough, especially when the door is opened and closed. Instead, store eggs in their carton, which not only helps keep them cold but also prevents them from picking up refrigerator odors. Additionally, eggs should be arranged with the broad ends up, which is how they are packed. This orientation keeps the yolk centered.

As eggs age, the whites will thin and become more transparent, and the yolks will flatten. Their nutritional value, however, does not change. But keep in mind that it is best to use fresh eggs for poaching, frying, or other recipes where they need to hold their shape.

## MAKING OMELETS

An omelet—beaten eggs cooked until firm, then folded, often around a filling—is a favorite breakfast dish. Shown opposite are the basic steps for making an omelet.

**1 Whisking the eggs:** Break the eggs called for in a recipe into a bowl. With a whisk, beat the eggs together with a little water, lemon juice (for a bright touch of acid flavor), and pinches of salt and freshly ground pepper until the color is even.

**2 Cooking the eggs:** Heat a nonstick frying pan over medium-high heat. Add the butter. The butter will foam, and when the foam begins to subside, pour the eggs through a sieve into the pan (this removes any white strands of albumen). As the eggs begin to set along the edges and bottom of the pan, carefully use a heatproof spatula to push the eggs slightly toward the center. Tilt the pan as necessary and work around the edges to allow the uncooked eggs to flow under the cooked portions.

**3 Adding the filling:** When the eggs in the center of the top are thickened and there is no more standing liquid, spoon the prepared filling, if using, over the half farthest from you.

**4 Folding the omelet:** Shake the pan gently to loosen the omelet. Using the spatula, lift up the half without the filling and turn it over the filling to make a half circle. Let the omelet cook for about 30 seconds longer, then gently slip it out onto a serving plate.

## BREAKFAST SPREADS AND TOPPINGS

*The following compote and sweetened butter add a special finishing touch to breads, pancakes, and waffles, while savory pesto may be used in omelets or other egg dishes.*

### SUMMER FRUIT COMPOTE

½ cup (4 oz/125 g) sugar

2 tablespoons water

1 mango, pitted and cut into ½-inch (12-mm) dice

2 ripe plums, pitted and cut into ½-inch (12-mm) dice

1 vanilla bean

In a small nonaluminum saucepan, bring the sugar and water to a boil over medium-high heat and boil until golden brown, about 6 minutes. Let cool for 5 minutes.

Meanwhile, place the mango and plums in a heatproof glass or ceramic bowl.

With a small, sharp knife, split the vanilla bean lengthwise and scrape out all the seeds with the tip of the knife. Add the seeds and the sugar syrup to the bowl. Let the compote steep for 20 minutes before serving. Makes about 3 cups (24 fl oz/750 ml).

*Serving Tip: This sweet and luscious compote is perfect on pancakes or waffles, and can be topped with a dollop of sweetened whipped cream for extra richness.*

### APPLE BUTTER

2½ lb (1.25 kg) Granny Smith apples

¾ cup (6 fl oz/180 ml) apple juice or cider

½ cup (3½ oz/105 g) firmly packed light brown sugar

½–¾ cup (4–6 oz/125–185 g) granulated sugar

½ teaspoon finely grated lemon zest

1 teaspoon ground cinnamon

⅛ teaspoon ground mace or nutmeg

⅛ teaspoon ground allspice

Quarter, core, and peel the apples. Combine the apples and apple juice in a large, non-aluminum saucepan. Bring to a boil over high heat. Reduce the heat to very low, cover, and simmer, stirring occasionally, until the apples are very soft, 20–30 minutes. Let stand, uncovered, for 10 minutes to cool slightly. In a blender or food processor, purée the mixture until smooth.

Preheat the oven to 325°F (165°C). Transfer the purée to a large roasting pan and stir in the brown sugar and ½ cup (4 oz/125 g) of the granulated sugar. Taste and add more granulated sugar if desired. Stir in the lemon zest, cinnamon, mace, and allspice. Bake uncovered, stirring occasionally, until the apple butter is thick, about 45 minutes.

Serve warm or cool. To store, place in airtight containers and refrigerate for up to 1 month. Makes about 3 cups (24 fl oz/750 ml).

*Serving Tip: Spread on toast, muffins, croissants, biscuits, or scones.*

### PESTO

2 tablespoons pine nuts

1 cup (8 fl oz/250 ml) extra-virgin olive oil

5 large cloves garlic, finely chopped

1 teaspoon salt

3 cups (3 oz/90 g) tightly packed basil leaves

⅓ cup (⅓ oz/10 g) coarsely chopped fresh spinach leaves (optional)

½ teaspoon freshly ground pepper

¼ cup (1 oz/30 g) grated best-quality Parmesan cheese

Preheat the oven to 350°F (180°C). Spread the pine nuts on a baking sheet in an even layer. Toast until slightly golden and aromatic, about 10 minutes. Remove from the oven and let cool to room temperature.

In a food processor, combine the olive oil, pine nuts, garlic, and salt. Pulse on and off, pausing to scrape down the sides, until smooth and creamy. Add the basil, spinach (if using), and pepper and process until smooth. Transfer to a glass or ceramic bowl and fold in the Parmesan. Makes about 2 cups (16 fl oz/500 ml).

*Tip: The pesto may be frozen, before the Parmesan is added, in an airtight container for up to 1 month. Before freezing, cover the pesto with a thin layer of olive oil to keep from discoloring. Thaw completely at room temperature before folding in the Parmesan.*

# BREAKFAST BEVERAGES

*Many people cannot open their eyes in the morning without the promise of a cup of coffee, while others thrive on tea. Still others shun caffeine in favor of fresh fruit juices. Whatever your choice, breakfast would be incomplete without a favorite beverage. For brunch gatherings, include a beverage with spirits as well as a caffeinated choice.*

## HOT CHOCOLATE

3 oz (90 g) best-quality, semisweet (plain) chocolate

¾ cup (6 fl oz/180 ml) boiling water

¾ cup (6 fl oz/180 ml) cup milk, or ½ cup (4 fl oz/125 ml) milk mixed with ¼ cup (2 fl oz/60 ml) heavy (double) cream

With a sharp knife, chop the chocolate into small pieces and place in a small saucepan. Pour a little of the boiling water over the chocolate and stir until the chocolate is melted. Add the remaining boiling water and the ¾ cup (6 fl oz/180 ml) cup milk; for an extra-rich drink, use the milk mixed with cream.

Set the pan over medium heat and, with a whisk, stir the mixture constantly, until hot but not boiling. Serve immediately in teacups, or set aside and reheat gently before serving. Makes 3 servings.

*Variation Tip: This rich hot chocolate may also be served in 6 demitasse cups.*

*Serving Tip: Serve with Almond-Currant Scones (page 82) or Brioche (page 86).*

## CHILLED SPICED COFFEE

1½ cups (12 fl oz/375 ml) freshly brewed coffee, hot

2 tablespoons sugar

1 tablespoon unsweetened Dutch-process cocoa powder

1 cinnamon stick, about 3 inches (7.5 cm) long

6 whole cloves

2 pieces orange zest, each about 3 inches (7.5 cm) long by 1 inch (2.5 cm) wide

Ice for serving (optional)

Milk or cream for serving (optional)

In a heatproof bowl or large, heatproof measuring pitcher, combine the coffee, sugar, and cocoa powder. Stir thoroughly to dissolve the sugar. Add the cinnamon stick and cloves. Twist each piece of orange zest to release the essential oils, then add to the hot liquid. Let stand at room temperature for 1 hour, stirring occasionally.

Pour through a strainer to remove the spices and zest, then cover and refrigerate until very cold. Stir well before serving. Serve cold or over ice and add a little milk or cream, if desired. Makes 2 servings.

*Serving Tip: Serve with Huevos Rancheros (page 52), Melon Salad with Yogurt-Honey Dressing (page 70), or Blueberry Muffins (page 78).*

## BLOODY MARY

Ice as needed

¼ cup (2 fl oz/60 ml) vodka

½ cup (4 fl oz/125 ml) tomato juice or V-8 juice

Juice of ½ lime, plus a lime wedge

1½ teaspoons Worcestershire sauce, or to taste

6 dashes hot-pepper sauce, or to taste

Salt and freshly ground pepper

Half fill a cocktail shaker with ice. Add the vodka, tomato juice, lime juice, Worcestershire sauce, hot-pepper sauce, and salt and pepper to taste. Shake briskly to combine.

Place a few ice cubes in a highball glass. Strain the Bloody Mary into the glass. Set the lime wedge on the rim of the glass and serve at once. Makes 1 serving.

*Serving Tip: Serve with Eggs Benedict (page 17) or Wild Mushroom Quiche (page 95).*

## TANGERINE JUICE AND PROSECCO

¼ cup (2 fl oz/60 ml) fresh tangerine juice, chilled

¾ cup (6 fl oz/180 ml) Italian Prosecco or other sparkling wine, chilled

Pour the tangerine juice into a champagne flute, top with the sparkling wine, and serve at once. Makes 1 serving.

*Serving Tip: Serve with Coddled Eggs with Chives and Cream (page 47), Goat Cheese and Spanish Ham Soufflé (page 96), or Broccoli Rabe, Pesto, and Smoked Mozzarella Strata (page 103).*

# GLOSSARY

BREAD CRUMBS, DRIED  To make dried bread crumbs, dry out slices of day-old French or other white bread in a 200°F (95°C) oven for about 1 hour. Break the bread into bite-sized pieces and process in a blender or food processor into fine crumbs. Dried bread crumbs will keep for up to 1 month in the refrigerator. For fresh bread crumbs, see page 66.

BUTTER  Butter is sold in two basic styles. More familiar is salted butter, but for cooking and baking, most recipes call for unsalted butter. Unsalted butter lacks the additional salt that can interfere with the taste of the final recipe, and it is also likely to be fresher since salt often acts as a preservative, prolonging butter's shelf life. For the best quality, seek out European-style butter, which contains less moisture and more flavorful butterfat. For spreading, you may want to use whipped butter, which has had air beaten into it and is lighter and easier to spread when cold.

CANADIAN BACON  Cut from the loin of the hog, and cured but not always smoked, Canadian bacon, also called back bacon, is generally sliced thick. Many people appreciate its mild flavor and lean, meaty texture, which are closer to that of ham than bacon. It is used for Eggs Benedict (page 17).

CHERVIL  A delicate springtime herb with curly, dark green leaves, chervil is best when used fresh in salads, with vegetables, or with eggs. It has a mild flavor reminiscent of parsley and anise.

CHIVES  The slender, bright green stems of chives are used to give an onionlike flavor without the bite. The hollow, grasslike leaves can be snipped with a pair of kitchen scissors to any length and scattered over scrambled eggs, coddled eggs, omelets, or any dish that could benefit from a boost of mild oniony flavor.

CILANTRO  Also called fresh coriander and Chinese parsley, cilantro is a distinctly flavored herb used extensively in Mexican, Asian, Indian, Latin, and Middle Eastern cuisines. It is best when added at the end of cooking; its flavor disappears during long exposure to heat. When shopping, do not confuse cilantro and flat-leaf (Italian) parsley, which look very similar and can be mistaken for each other.

CRÈME FRAÎCHE  See page 99.

DOUBLE BOILER  A specialized set of pans used for gentle cooking, a double boiler consists of one pan nested atop another with room for water to simmer in the lower pan. The top pan should not touch the water in the lower pan, and the water should never boil. A tight fit between the pans ensures that no water or steam mixes with the ingredients. If you don't have a double boiler, choose a heatproof bowl that fits snugly on top of a saucepan and nest the two together.

EGG, RAW  Eggs are sometimes used raw or partially cooked in sauces and other preparations. These eggs run a risk of being infected with salmonella or other bacteria, which can lead to food poisoning. This risk is of most concern to small children, older people, pregnant women, and anyone with a compromised immune system. If you have health and safety concerns, do not consume undercooked egg, or seek out a pasteurized egg product to replace it. Eggs can also be made safe by heating them to a temperature of 140°F (60°C) for 3½ minutes. Note that coddled, poached, and soft-boiled eggs are often undercooked.

EGGS, SEPARATING  See page 96.

FARMER'S CHEESE  This white, fresh cheese is a form of cottage cheese from which most of the liquid has been removed. It is sold in a fairly solid loaf shape and is mild and slightly tangy.

GRUYÈRE  This smooth, creamy cow's milk cheese is produced in Switzerland

and France. It is revered for its nutty yet mild flavor and firm texture and is wonderful for melting.

LEEKS, RINSING  Because leeks grow partly underground, often in sandy soil, grit can be lodged between the layers of their leaves. For this reason, it is important to rinse leeks before use in a recipe. Trim off the roots and cut off and discard the tough, dark green tops. If the outer layer is wilted or discolored, peel it away and discard. Quarter or halve the stalk lengthwise, leaving the long layers attached at the root end. Hold the leek under cold running water, separating the layers to wash away any dirt.

OATS  Rich, robust, and flavorful, this favorite grain of northern Europe, Scotland, and Ireland is enjoyed in many forms: old-fashioned rolled oats, quick-cooking oats, instant oats, and steel-cut oats.

Old-fashioned rolled oats are whole oats that have been steamed and rolled to make them flat. Quick-cooking oats are cut into smaller pieces before steaming and rolling so they cook faster. Instant oats are precooked, are cut even smaller than quick-cooking oats, and often have added salt, sugar, and flavorings. Steel-cut oats, also called Scotch oats or Irish oatmeal, aren't rolled at all. Instead, they are cut into two or three pieces. Some people prefer to use steel-cut oats, but they take longer to cook and have a chewier texture.

Oats start out quite large, and the more an oat is cut, the more perishable it becomes.

Unless you plan to serve hot oatmeal regularly, buy only as much oats as you plan to use within a few weeks.

PEPPER, WHITE  Made from peppercorns that have had their skins removed and berries dried, white pepper is often less aromatic and more mild in flavor than black pepper. It is favored in the preparation of light-colored sauces when cooks want to avoid flecks of black pepper in the final dish.

SEA SALT  Unlike standard table salt, sea salt has no additives. It does have more minerals and is naturally evaporated rather than evaporated in vacuum pans, the process by which table salt is made. Sea salt is available in coarse or fine grains that are shaped like hollow, flaky pyramids. As a result, it adheres better to foods and dissolves more quickly than table salt. Sea salt also has more flavor than table salt, and sometimes a smaller amount is sufficient to season the same amount of food.

WHISKS  With a head of looped thin metal wires, a whisk is used to rapidly beat or whip ingredients. Also known as whips, whisks are made in various sizes and shapes for various uses. Elongated sauce whisks are the basic model and are used to mix ingredients thoroughly without adding excess air. Balloon

whisks, which are more rounded, are used to incorporate the maximum amount of air when whipping egg whites and cream.

WILD MUSHROOMS  The distinction between wild and cultivated mushrooms has grown somewhat blurred as varieties once found only in the wild are now farmed. Nevertheless, a number of mushrooms have resisted cultivation, including chanterelles, with their distinctive trumpet shape and apricot-flavored overtones; porcini, whose large caps have an earthy flavor; and shiitakes, which have plump caps possessing a meaty texture. Cremini are light brown in color and have a firmer texture and fuller flavor than common white mushrooms.

ZESTER  A handheld tool with a row of circular holes at the end of its metal blade, specially designed to remove zest from citrus efficiently. For citrus zest, choose organic fruit if possible and be sure to scrub the fruit well to remove any wax or residue. Cut off only the thin, colored portion of the rind, taking care not to include the bitter white pith. A vegetable peeler or a paring knife can also be used, but often produces pieces that are short but wide and need further slicing. Zest may be removed with the fine rasps of a handheld grater as well.

# INDEX

SIMON & SCHUSTER SOURCE
A Division of Simon & Schuster, Inc.
1230 Avenue of the Americas
New York, NY 10020

WILLIAMS-SONOMA
Founder and Vice-Chairman: Chuck Williams

WELDON OWEN INC.
Chief Executive Officer: John Owen
President: Terry Newell
Chief Operating Officer: Larry Partington
Vice President, International Sales: Stuart Laurence
Creative Director: Gaye Allen
Series Editor: Sarah Putman Clegg
Editor: Heather Belt
Designer: Teri Gardiner
Production: Chris Hemesath and Teri Bell
Production Assistant: Libby Temple

Weldon Owen wishes to thank the following
people for their generous assistance and support
in producing this book: Copy Editor Carrie Bradley;
Consulting Editors Sharon Silva and Judith Dunham;
Food Stylists Kim Konecny and Erin Quon;
Photographer's Assistant Faiza Ali;
Proofreaders Desne Ahlers and Linda Bouchard;
Indexer Ken DellaPenta; and
Production Designer Joan Olson.

Set in Trajan, Utopia, and Vectora.

Williams-Sonoma Collection *Breakfast* was
conceived and produced by Weldon Owen Inc.,
814 Montgomery Street, San Francisco,
California 94133, in collaboration with
Williams-Sonoma, 3250 Van Ness Avenue,
San Francisco, California 94109.

A Weldon Owen Production
Copyright © 2003 by Weldon Owen Inc. and
Williams-Sonoma Inc.

For information about special discounts for bulk
purchases, please contact Simon & Schuster
Special Sales: 1-800-456-6798 or
business@simonandschuster.com

Color separations by Bright Arts Graphics
Singapore (Pte.) Ltd.
Printed and bound in Singapore by Tien Wah
Press (Pte.) Ltd.

First printed in 2003.

10 9 8 7

Library of Congress Cataloging-in-Publication
Data is available.

ISBN 13: 978-0-7432-4366-7

**A NOTE ON WEIGHTS AND MEASURES**

All recipes include customary U.S. and metric measurements. Metric conversions are based on
a standard developed for these books and have been rounded off. Actual weights may vary.